Aana
Mansala

Tempest In A Teapot: Recipes and Reminiscence

Sara Marsala

iUniverse, Inc.
New York Bloomington

Tempest In A Teapot: Recipes and Reminiscence

Copyright © 2008 bySara Marsala

iUniverse books may be ordered through booksellers or by contacting:

iUniverse
1663 Liberty Drive
Bloomington, IN 47403
www.iuniverse.com
1-800-Authors (1-800-288-4677)

ISBN: 978-0-595-52370-2 (pbk)
ISBN: 978-0-595-51573-8 (cloth)
ISBN: 978-0-595-62427-0 (ebk)

Printed in the United States of America

Foreword

I wished to write this book to honour my customers and tea room enthusiasts everywhere.

There is something quite magical about tea rooms. They transcend time and place, evoking a sense of gentility and grace. Traditionally tea rooms were one of the first places where an unaccompanied woman could go to meet a friend for a cup of coffee or tea. Today, though men certainly enjoy them too, it is mostly women who flock to these institutions to experience the sense of beauty, elegance and friendship of a bygone era. It is this nostalgia, combined with my love of baking that first led me to open a tea room. I wanted very much to create a space where one could go to escape the madness of everyday life. A sanctuary, if you will, where the cares of the day could be dispelled with a wonderfully fragrant cup of tea and a sweet something to accompany it, in an atmosphere that was serene and soothing.

I share with you my love and knowledge of tea, from its rich, storied history, to the way it is produced. It is a beverage that has successfully stood the test of time. Revered in many cultures, it is more widely popular today than it ever was in the past. You will learn about the enduring custom of afternoon tea, a treasure in its own right, enjoyed throughout Britain and in tea rooms around the world. For millennia, people have come together over food, and it is my hope that these recipes will generate great memories for you to share with your loved ones for years to come.

I share with you also the special Reminiscence of my tea room, *Tempest in a Teapot*. I opened my doors to strangers and they left as friends. The short stories told within these pages are actual occurrences of events that my customers have kindly shared with me or that I have witnessed. They are written in the third person, because that is how I am most comfortable writing, but the spirit of these events is true. I have however, changed some of the names and added fictional details to them in order to convey the essence of the occasion, be it a celebration, a reconciling or a respite. These were events that touched my heart and validated my reasons for opening a tea room; a place of gathering to celebrate life's happenings, large or small.

I wish to thank the wonderful people who worked with me, who helped me realize my dream. I could not have done it without you. There were certainly challenges along the way, but such is life. To my many friends who have given me support through my adventure, and have offered a sounding board for my ideas, thank you, thank you, thank you!

To my husband Robert, and my sons Paul and Adam, I give gratitude and love. They fuelled my dream, helped me set up a business, move a business and close a business.

Lastly, if success is measured by memories made and held in the hearts of my customers; by friendships made and nurtured, then I was successful. Thank you.

Sara Marsala
2008

Contents

Introduction

Say the word 'tea' and it is likely to mean different things to different people. While it is both a beverage and a meal, it is certain to evoke pleasurable feelings in either case. As a beverage, it not only quenches our thirst, but offers warmth and comfort after a wet soggy day and soothes after a stressful day. It is a celebration meal, and repast with good friends or a consoling occasion after a misfortune. Many people start the day with it, have it with their meals and enjoy a cup at days end. It is enjoyed steaming hot or ice cold, alone or with company. Is it any wonder that it's the second most popular beverage in the world after water?

Chapter One
Tea – The Beverage

"A sip of this will bathe the drooping spirits in delight, beyond the bliss of dreams."

John Milton

Tea has been around forever. So long, in fact, that its origins have been cloaked in myth and legend. It is commonly believed to have been the Chinese, some 5000 years ago, who first discovered it. Legend has it that Emperor and herbalist Shen Nung, also known as the Divine Healer, liked to have his drinking water boiled for hygienic purposes as he believed that this contributed to longevity. One day, while sitting around a camp site, leaves from a nearby bush fell into his freshly boiled water and the Emperor noted a pleasant colour and taste – thus tea was discovered.

For many years, tea production in China was a closely guarded secret. It was certainly the national drink of China by the time of the Tang Dynasty, from 618 to 906 AD. It was during this dynasty that the practice developed of sending the finest teas to the emperor's court in his honour. At this time, tea trading also began with India, Turkey and Russia. Though it became widely available in other parts of the world, the history of tea in China and Japan is historically more significant as it was infused with literary, artistic and even religious overtones. This can be traced, in part, to the writings of a Chinese scholar called Lu Yu, who in the eighth century wrote a detailed essay called the Ch'a Ching, the Classic of Tea. This was credited as being the single most influential aspect in developing the cultural importance of tea. It elevated the preparation and drinking of tea to near religious status where there were guidelines on the acceptable state of mind for the tea drinker and the atmosphere in which tea should be drunk. This coincided with the Taoist faith at the time which believed that every detail of life was worthy of celebration, and that one should attempt to find beauty everywhere. This emphasis on tranquility and harmony in the preparation and drinking of tea has endured through the ages.

From its innocuous beginning, today tea has evolved to a multi-billion dollar plantation crop. All tea comes from the *Camellia Sinensis* plant which is indigenous to China, Tibet, and northern India. It has been successfully cultivated in other parts of the world as well. Today, tea plantations cover about 6 million acres of land with India being the world's leading producer. The plant, which can grow to the height of 90 feet and more in the wild, is pruned every four or five years in order to rejuvenate the bush and keep it at a height of three feet for cultivation purposes. This is a convenient height for pluckers to pick the tea from, and is known as the "Plucking Table". Tea pluckers remove the top two leaves and buds of new shoots at intervals of 7 – 12 days during the growing season. This harvesting is labour intensive as two to three thousand tea leaves are required to produce one kilo of unprocessed tea. The pluckers rely on their considerable skill to recognize the exact moment when the flush (or first harvest) should be removed in order to ensure that the most tender leaves are plucked to produce the finest teas. A tea bush can produce tea for 50 – 70 years, but usually becomes less productive after 50 years, at which time the bush is replaced by plants grown on the estate. The tea estate, or tea garden, is where the flavour characteristics will be generated. The vast variety of teas available are a result of subtle influences of soil conditions, climate, altitude and processing, which play a vital role, and therefore great care and attention is taken to insure that the best possible growing conditions are created. Not unlike wines, often teas take their name from the district they are grown - Assam, Darjeeling and Ceylon being some of the most recognized teas.

Though there are many varieties of teas now available worldwide, all teas can be divided into three main categories – **black, oolong and green.**

Black tea is fully oxidized tea. Oxidation, otherwise known as fermentation is a complicated chemical reaction that occurs when the tea leaves react with the air and begin to break down. Ultimately it is this reaction that creates the different types of tea.

Black tea is made by gathering the top two leaves and bud of the tea plant. These are then transported to the factory, usually adjacent to the fields, where they are withered. This involves spreading the leaves out on long bamboo trays in warm temperatures for 12 – 16 hours until they lose approximately 50% - 70% of their moisture (this varies from region to region). The withered leaves are then rolled, crushed, torn and curled to break open the tea cells which allows the natural juices or enzymes to be released, and on contact with air will oxidize. The broken leaf is laid out again in trays in a cool, humid environment for three to four hours and is turned over repeatedly until the leaves turn a golden colour and oxidation is complete. After oxidation the leaf is dried or fired by passing the broken leaf slowly through hot air chambers where any remaining moisture will be evaporated and the leaf turns a dark brown or black. The black tea is ejected from the hot chamber into chests. After this the tea is sorted, tasted and blended or flavoured. Black tea is characterized by its hearty, deep flavour and dark colour.

Oolong tea is often referred to as a cross between a black tea and a green tea because it is only partially oxidized. The leaves are wilted in direct sunlight to evaporate moisture; then tossed in baskets in order to lightly bruise the edges of the leaf, which allows only a portion of the enzymes to be exposed to air. The leaves are then steamed to further stop oxidation. After that, a final drying takes place before they are sent to be sorted, graded and packaged. It should be noted that oolong teas have varying degrees of oxidation that can range from 15% – 75%. It is this vast variation that makes this the most complicated tea to produce and requires experienced and skilled craftsmen to create the enormous range of flavors and fragrances available. Additionally, oolong teas are normally dried at higher temperatures, and thus contain less moisture, so they therefore have a longer shelf life than green teas. This type of tea is processed to be full bodied, is therefore extremely flavourful and highly aromatic and is best enjoyed without milk or sugar.

Green tea is unoxidized or unfermented tea. It may or may not go through a withering process. The leaves are immediately pan fired, steamed or baked to prevent oxidization, then rolled and dried. Green teas are characterized by their delicate taste and pale green colour.

White tea is a sub category of green tea, and is the most delicate of all teas. The new buds are plucked before they open in the early spring, withered so that the natural moisture evaporates and then dried slowly at low temperatures. White tea is also unoxidized, is the least processed of all teas, and has a mild flavour and natural sweetness.

Herbals and Tisanes are not real teas, in that they do not come from the camellia sinensis plant but bear mentioning here. They contain no real tea in them, and for this reason they are naturally caffeine free and are a good alternative for those who are sensitive to caffeine. They are a blend of herbs, leaves, flowers, spices, berries or dried fruit chunks. Although sugar can be added to herbal teas, they are best enjoyed without. I do not recommend milk be added to herbals, especially if they contain any dried fruit pieces as this sometimes causes the milk to curdle.

Rooibos tea is another type of herbal tea. It is not blended, but is made with the needle-like leaves of the *Aspalathus Linearis* plant that grows in the wild in South Africa. It is sometimes referred to as 'South African red tea', or 'red bush tea' as Rooibos literally means red bush in the Afrikaans language. It has been enjoyed by the South Africans for generations and is now consumed in many countries.

For many years, black tea in tea bags has been the most commonly available tea in North America. Thankfully that has slowly been changing as tea seems to be enjoying a re-birth of sorts. Although always popular, it has seen a dramatic increase in consumption due, in part, to the scientific research on health benefits associated with drinking tea. Also, new flavoured varieties, better marketing and a health conscious population have combined to make it the beverage of choice for many people.

HOW TO MAKE A GREAT POT OF TEA

BLACK TEA AND OOLONG TEA
- Use filtered cold water and bring to a rolling boil.
- Warm the teapot with hot tap water while your kettle is boiling. This helps keep your tea hot longer. Just before your water comes to the boil, drain the hot tap water from your teapot and add your tea.
- Use one teaspoonful of loose tea or one single serving teabag per cup of water. If you are using a four cup teapot, add 4 teaspoons of loose tea or 4 teabags.
- Pour the boiling water over the tea leaves in the pot.
- Cover and steep black tea for 3 to 5 minutes to ensure maximum flavour. Steep oolong tea for 3 – 8 minutes.
- Strain tea or remove teabags.

GREEN TEA AND WHITE TEA
- Use filtered cold water and bring it to a rolling boil.
- Next, allow the water to cool to a temperature somewhere between 165-185° before you pour it over the tea leaves. (Let the boiled water sit for between 30 and 60 seconds to cool to this temperature.)

- Warm the teapot with hot tap water while your kettle is boiling. This helps keep your tea hot longer. While you are waiting for your boiled water to cool slightly, drain the hot tap water from your teapot and add your tea.
- Use one teaspoonful of loose tea or one single serving teabag per cup of water. If you are using a four cup teapot, add 4 teaspoons of loose tea or 4 teabags.
- Pour the slightly cooled water over the tea leaves in the pot.
- Cover and steep green tea for 3 - 4 minutes only. Steep white tea for 4 – 8 minutes.
- Strain tea or remove teabags.

FRESH BREWED ICED TEA

- Place 6 teaspoons of loose leaf tea or 6 tea bags into a one litre pitcher.
- Pour 1 1/4 cups (300 ml) of freshly boiled water over tea bags in pitcher. Steep for five minutes. Strain tea or remove tea bags. Fill pitcher with fresh cold water.
- Pour over ice. Garnish and sweeten to taste.
- Fresh, brewed iced tea should be stored in the refrigerator.

HERBAL TEAS

Herbal infusions are prepared similarly to black teas.
- Use filtered cold water and bring it to a rolling boil.
- Steep the herbs for approximately 5 minutes or more. The longer herbs steep, the more intense their flavor. You may remove the herbs when they reach your desired taste, or leave them in to strengthen the flavors (a stronger brew makes a better iced tea).

Times given are only guidelines. You may prefer a weaker or stronger tea. Adjust steeping time accordingly.

TEAS TO ENJOY

In the Tea Room, we sold about 48 different teas. My only regret is that we did not have the space to carry more as there are literally hundreds and hundreds of teas and varieties from all around the world with unique flavour characteristics. If you have the opportunity of tasting different teas, take advantage and try them out. If you are not already a tea enthusiast, I am convinced you will soon be one after sampling some of the wonderful teas that are now available. Below is a listing of some of the most requested teas that we sold. I urge you to give them a try!

Estate Teas

Lover's Leap: this is an estate tea from the Dimbula area of Sri Lanka. Its flavour is somewhat light making it an excellent choice for those who do not prefer a strong or flavoured tea.

Margaret's Hope: from one of Darjeeling's best known estates, this tea has a lovely muscatel flavour with a delicious astringency.

China Black Teas

Lapsang Souchong: this tea has a heady aroma of a smoky pine and oak wood fire. No in-betweens with this tea, either love it or hate it!

Keemun Panda: a winey, fruity tea with depth and complexity. Rewards the tea drinker with an exotic cup tending bright and reddish.

Naturally Flavoured Black Teas

Ginger: Piquant, spicy and fruity. Very refreshing!

Maple Cream: Exquisite maple tea with sweet caramel flavour notes and a twist of creamy smoothness.

Vanilla Cream: Rich fresh vanilla and a lovely cream character.

English Favorites

Buckingham Palace Garden Party: Medium body tea. Delicate Earl Grey and Jasmine notes.

Cream Earl Grey: More popular than the regular Earl Grey, this tea has a rich creaminess and aroma that must be tasted. Our most popular tea hands down!

Irish Breakfast: A stout robust tea with superb colour and great body. Excellent early in the day!

Windsor Castle: Full bodied flavour, this tea has toasty notes from Darjeeling and lively flavour from Ceylon.

Green Teas

Sencha: Classic green tea, smooth tasting with light colour.

Sencha Kyoto Cherry Rose: A base of classic green sencha with sweet cherry and morning rose flavour.

Jasmine: Exquisite jasmine character on a seasonal green tea.

Rooibos

Bourbon St. Vanilla: Vanilla flavour and almond flakes make this rooibos naturally sweet and caramelly.

Provence: Floral notes from the lavender, and fruity notes from the dried currants. Inspired by the 'joie de vivre' of France.

Herbal Fruit Teas

Angel Falls Mist: A wildly exotic mix of strawberry and lemon.

Cranberry Apple: Full flavoured and pungent with a rich, fruity character. Add a cinnamon stick or a few cloves for an exotic mulled spiced tea.

THE HEALTH BENEFITS OF TEA

"Drinking a daily cup of tea will surely starve the apothecary."

Chinese Proverb

Over the last twenty years alone, researchers and government health agencies around the world have conducted many scientific studies on tea and its potential health benefits. This research has found that tea offers some protection from cardiovascular disease, cancer, aids in the reduced risk of developing kidney stones, and strengthens bones, teeth and the immune system. The scientific data to support these claims are complicated to understand and are beyond the realm of this book, so I will only be discussing this subject in a general way. I urge you to do your own research on the subject if it is something that interests you.

Tea contains no fat, calories or salt, but is rich in naturally occurring flavonoids which are very effective antioxidants. These protect cells from damage caused by free radicals and other carcinogens, by flushing out the bad while maintaining normal cell growth. We already know that antioxidant rich foods play a role in reducing the risk of certain types of cancers, heart disease or stroke. The antioxidant activity in two cups of tea is equal to drinking seven glasses of orange juice or eating 4 apples. Therefore, when aiming for a healthy lifestyle, the antioxidant value alone in tea is certainly worth considering.

TEA AND VITAMINS

All tea, black, green, white and oolong contain measurable amount of the following:

Zinc – shown to boost the immune system

Folic Acid – helps the body to make healthy new cells

Manganese – is needed for healthy skin, bone and cartilage formation

Potassium - works with sodium to maintain the body's water balance

Vitamin C - stimulates the immune system and acts as an antioxidant

TEA AND CAFFEINE

Caffeine is classified as a stimulant because it increases the activity of the cardiovascular system, digestive system, and provides a sense of alertness in the brain. It accounts for tea's energizing qualities and has been shown to speed reaction time and improve concentration. While too much caffeine has been associated with negative health benefits, it is important to remember that caffeine tolerance varies greatly among individuals. Pound for pound, loose tea leaves and ground coffee contain similar levels of caffeine; however, one pound of tea leaves yields roughly 200 cups of tea, while a pound of coffee yields roughly 60 cups of coffee. The result is that caffeine content in tea is about 1/3 less than that found in coffee. There are several other factors that affect the content of caffeine in tea and these bear mentioning:

- Steeping time
o   The longer tea is steeped the higher the content of caffeine, which starts to release after about one minute of steeping. If you want to decrease the amount of caffeine in your tea, slightly increase the amount of tea leaves, while decreasing the steeping time.

- Tea leaf size
  - The smaller the tea leaf the stronger extraction of caffeine. Teabags release up to twice as much caffeine as loose teas because they are made with low grade leaves that are crushed up. As soon as a tea leaf is crushed, the surface area of the leaf is exposed to more air, which causes the tea to lose nutrients and flavour. To counteract this, more crushed leaves are used, which equals more caffeine.
- Tea leaf location
  - The first and second leaves of the tea plant are believed to contain the largest amount of caffeine.
- Fermentation
  - The longer the leaves have fermented, the greater the caffeine content. Therefore black teas normally contain more caffeine than oolong or green tea.

Chapter Two
Tea – The Meal

*"There are few hours in life more agreeable than the hour dedicated to
the ceremony known as afternoon tea."*

Henry James

In Britain, tea was first popularized by Catherine of Braganza, (1638-1705)
the queen of Charles II. She had enjoyed tea since her childhood in Portugal,
and brought tea drinking to the royal court where she set a trend for the
beverage among the aristocracy of England. It soon became a popular drink
in the London coffee houses where businessmen met to discuss the events of
the day. At this time, tea was heavily taxed, which made it a very expensive
beverage confined to wealthier households. Despite its high price, the British
became enthusiastic tea drinkers. There was, however, a clear gap between
the masses who wanted to drink tea, and the relatively few who could afford
to do so. This gap was soon filled by tea smugglers, who paid no duty on it,
and could sell it for much cheaper. It was estimated that these sophisticated
smuggling networks smuggled in more tea than was brought in legally. This
had a very important consequence for tea drinking; because it made tea more
affordable, the beverage became more popular among all sections of society,
and became an integral part of everyday life. Soon the government, under
pressure from legal tea merchants whose profits were being eroded by the

smugglers, cut the duty on tea which further contributed in bringing tea to the working classes.

While tea was becoming part of the regular diet of the poor, among the rich, tea drinking was evolving into an elaborate social affair. We owe the pleasure of afternoon tea to the Victorians, specifically to Anna, Seventh Duchess of Bedford (1788-1861). At this time, Victorians enjoyed two main meals of the day; breakfast and dinner. They normally ate a large first meal of ale, bread and beef early in the day. Dinner was a long, hearty meal late at night, and there was not likely to be much between. Anna began ordering a small meal of bread, butter and tea in the afternoon in order to keep her going until the heavy evening meal was served. It was to be secretly delivered to her boudoir where she would sometimes invite friends to join her. The Duchess' summer practice proved very popular and was continued when she returned to London. There too, the idea caught on and the concept of a small meal served with tea became very trendy, and came to be known as Afternoon Tea.

Soon this quaint custom evolved to an occasion for hats, gloves and Sunday best attire. Hostesses were judged, not only on the food they presented, but also on the proper tea accoutrements such as strainers, sugar tongs and napkins. Books on etiquette and good housekeeping of that time document how to conduct a correct afternoon tea. The table would often be embellished with flowers and draped in fine linens, laden with delicate foods and sweet treats served up in the finest bone china. Afternoon Tea was frequently an elaborate affair and became the perfect finale to an afternoon wedding or christening celebration. Poorer households, always imitating the rich, began to hold afternoon teas. The women would pool their resources and equipment together in order to make this more affordable.

In its simplest form Afternoon Tea consists of a selection of small sandwiches; crust on or off, scones with cream and jam, and small dainty desserts. Generally speaking, North Americans mistakenly refer to this meal as High Tea. Traditionally, High Tea in Britain was served at dinner time and would include heartier fare like Sheppard's pie or other meat pies or pasties. This was, in essence, a working man's dinner and was served at the kitchen table, or high table, hence its name. In contrast, afternoon tea was mostly served in the parlour on lower tables, and was sometimes referred to as Low Tea.

While tea was gaining popularity as a meal, tea rooms began to be established. The forerunner of these was perhaps the coffee houses. These had been long established as meeting places for men exclusively and were often called "Penny Universities" because they offered a place where men could get a cup of coffee, and later tea, a copy of the newspaper and engage in conversation with the some of the most intelligent men of the day. While coffee houses were popular among men, they were no place for women as they also sold liquor. Ladies who wanted to purchase tea for consumption at home would either rely on their husbands to do this for them, or send their footmen. Soon they began to demand better service. This call for change fell on the ears of coffee house proprietor Thomas Twinning, who converted his coffee house and neighbouring properties into a dry tea and coffee shop where ladies were welcome.

At the same time, the English developed the idea of Tea Gardens, which were modeled after the Dutch "tavern garden teas". These were outdoor tea venues where gentlemen took their ladies to enjoy music and tea. Often on private lands, these were open only during the summer and admission was charged to gain entrance. Here women were allowed to mix freely for the first time without social criticism. They became social melting pots were the classes conjoined for an afternoons outing. Incidentally, it is believed that the custom of tipping was first created at these tea gardens. Small locked boxes were placed on the tables throughout the gardens. Inscribed on each of these were the letters T.I.P.S. which stood for "To Insure Prompt Service". If a guest wanted to make sure he was promptly served, he would drop a coin in the box on being seated.

The combination of coffee house and tea garden led to the contemporary tea rooms that are now frequented throughout Europe and North America, and where typically, Afternoon tea is mostly enjoyed as a special treat. Not usually prepared at home, unless it is to host a small birthday or shower, most people prefer to experience Afternoon Tea at a tea room or hotel. While there is nothing like the luxury of being waited on, Afternoon Tea prepared at home can be a simple, casual affair, with food made up in advance and waiting in the refrigerator until your guests arrive. It you don't have the time to prepare a full Afternoon Tea, you can certainly very easily enjoy a Cream Tea. This is a smaller meal, more of a snack really, and is nothing more than scones with jam and cream, and tea, sometimes a shortbread cookie on the side.

Cream Teas are said to have started in Devon, home of the famous Devon cream. It is thought that around the year 1105, the monks of the Benedictine Abbey in Tavistock liked to reward local workers, who were restoring the Abbey, with bread, clotted cream and strawberry preserves. After the Abbey was completely restored the monks continued serving these cream treats to passing travelers. While it may be true that the custom of bread or scones with jam and cream was initially started in Devon, they most certainly would have had to serve this with a beverage other than tea, as it was not introduced into Europe until the 1600's.

The essence of Afternoon Tea is really more important than what is served or how it is presented. Casual or fussy, planned weeks in advance or at the spur of the moment, whether it is served in the comfort of your living room, or experienced in a well-appointed tea room, it should always be pleasurable. Just like the Chinese and Japanese believed many years ago, it should be a time of tranquility and harmony – a time to de-compress, unwind, breathe. So, enjoy a great cup of tea on your own or in the company of your closest, dearest friends, whatever suits your mood.

Give yourself the gift of Afternoon Tea!

Chapter Three
Reminiscence
Scones and other Teatime treats

Chloe tugged at the skirt of her pale green dress, feeling slightly foolish and hoping that she would not run into anybody she knew. She would never in a million years get this dressed up to go out with her friends, and she supposed they would think her silly if they could see her now, but she did so want to make a good impression on her grandmother. Her father's mother, grandma Joan, had been a huge part of her life when she was younger, but her parent's divorce five years ago, had strained the relationship. Chloe was never entirely sure if it was her grandmother who stopped coming around, or if it was her mother who had kept her grandmother away. She would never understand the intricacies of adult relationships, but she was certainly glad her grandmother had come back to her. Grandma Joan had made an unannounced appearance at their house two weeks ago, and after a private and hushed conversation with her mother and step-father in the kitchen, Chloe and her brother had been called in to say hello. They spent the next two hours catching up, with Grandma asking them all sorts of questions about school and their hobbies and friends, and Chloe countered back with questions of her own. "Have you been on lots of traveling adventures like you used to?" She had asked of her grandmother. Grandma Joan had become very quiet. No, she had said, she had not been well for a time, but was feeling much better now.

A week after that, Chloe had received a personally addressed envelope in the mail from her grandmother. She had been invited to Tea on the 24th, and would Chloe be free to join her. Chloe had never been 'to tea' before, well not in real life anyway, and was not really sure of what to do and how to act. She had spent the next week obsessing about what to wear. Her mother had suggested that maybe her low rise jeans were not dressy enough and perhaps she should wear the green dress she had worn for her cousin's wedding earlier in the year. Chloe said she would think about it, but it was not likely. She had never really liked that dress.

Now, sitting in the tea room with her grandmother, wearing the hated green dress, Chloe finally started to relax. It hadn't been that bad. So far she hadn't run into anybody she knew. Her friends were all going to the movies this afternoon. She was beginning to feel a little guilty as she thought about her conversation with her friends this morning when she had told them she wasn't free to go with them because she had to go out with her grandmother. "Whatever!" she had told them, as if tea with her grandma was something Chloe had been forced to do, and would certainly not enjoy. To be honest, she was a little confused about the whole thing. She had always loved playing tea when she was younger, and when her grandmother gave her her first real tea set, Chloe had been thrilled. She had spent many happy times "taking tea" with her teddy bear, Max. It had been such fun to "pour" and hand out the little mini-cakes she had made in her Easy Bake oven. But it was somehow different now. She was twelve, not a baby anymore, and she certainly did not know of any other twelve years old who went to tea.

Grandma Joan had gotten her hair done for the occasion and was looking very nice, even if she did look a little thinner than she used to. From across the table, her grandmother smiled at her with those crystal clear blue eyes that Chloe vividly remembered from her childhood, and she was filled with a sense of happiness. She had not realized, until now, just how much she had missed her grandmother, and her smiling blue eyes and her laughter. Chloe reached out to touch her grandmother's hand. Her skin was surprisingly soft and her hand was quite small. She realized for the first time just how fragile her grandmother was, and was suddenly filled with sadness. Her grandmother squeezed her hand tightly and her crinkled eyes got a little bit misty. "You have certainly grown up to be a lovely young woman, Chloe," she said as they waited for their tea. "And that dress looks great on you. It brings out the green in your eyes."

When the tea arrived at the table, Chloe was momentarily struck by panic. She looked at the table and wondered where to start. What were the silver mesh things and what were they used for? They reminded Chloe of a miniature version of the strainer her mother used to strain the pasta out of its water. What if she spilled the tea, or dropped her teacup? What if she made a fool of herself and her grandmother would be disappointed? That was silly, she reasoned with herself, just calm down. She watched carefully as her grandmother started. She first took the silver mesh strainer and placed it on top of her teacup, then lifted the teapot and poured her tea. Brown bits fell out of the teapot along with the brown liquid and collected in the mesh. Chloe had never seen tea like this before. Her grandmother removed the strainer, with its bit of brown leaves, and replaced it on its base. She then added sugar and milk to her teacup. Chloe braced herself and tried to repeat her grandmother's actions. Lift it slowly, remember the strainer, and pour it carefully. Sweet, she really could do this! It was just like playing 'tea' so many years ago when her mother had filled the pot with juice. She sipped her tea slowly making sure to take just a small sip at a time as she knew the tea would be hot.

When the three tiered tea tray was being carried across the room to their table, Chloe's eyes rounded and she almost gasped out loud. There were lots of tiny desserts and lemon tarts, and chocolate strawberries and mini sandwiches cut in squares and triangles, and small biscuit looking things. Where to start? Where to start? Her grandmother smiled and winked at her from across the table. Chloe winked back. She took another sip of the sweet tea and waited again for her grandmother to make the first move. She carefully mirrored her grandmother's actions and started with a small, delicate sandwich. It was good. She ate it up and tentatively selected another. She was getting the hang of this. After a time, all the sandwiches were eaten up and Chloe boldly chose the biscuit looking thing before her grandmother. "Aren't the scones lovely, dear?" asked her grandmother, as she spread cream and jam on hers. Scones, was that was they were called? Chloe had already started to eat hers without the cream and jam; in fact, it was mostly all in her mouth already. She gulped, swallowed and washed it down with tea. She wondered if anybody noticed that she hadn't got it right. But no one seemed to be paying much attention to what she and her grandmother were doing; they were all talking and enjoying their own food.

"You know," her grandmother said, "I couldn't eat another bite of this delicious scone if I'm going to enjoy these fabulous little desserts. Would you like to finish this half of my scone, Chloe?" Chloe hesitated. She did not want to seem like a little pig, always stuffing food down her face, but she did so want to taste the scone with the cream and jam. "Yes, please," she found herself saying before she was even aware of it. She carefully spread first the cream; then the jam on the scone just like her grandmother had done, and took a bite. It was out of this world! She thought it was really good plain, but it was awesome all slathered up. She was certainly glad she hadn't missed it. And, she would know how to do it right the next time. Next time.....she thought to herself. She certainly hoped there would be a next time as she looked at her grandmother affectionately. She hoped there would be many next times. She could hardly wait to text her friends about it. Maybe they could join her some time. No, she decided, she liked her friends and all, but Chloe really wanted this to be just for her and her grandmother. It would be their special time together. She had missed her grandmother far too much to share her with her friends.

Chloe smiled at her grandmother across the table and winked. Not so bad, this 'tea' thing. Not so bad at all.

RECIPES

SCONES AND OTHER TEA TIME TREATS

"Come along inside, we'll see if tea and buns can make the world a better place."

Wind in the Willows, Kenneth Grahame

1. Sweet Scones

2. Lemon Curd

3. Shortbread in Two variations

4. Empire Cookies

5. Old fashioned Lemon Tarts

6. Orange Madeleines

7. Mini Lemon Coconut Cupcakes

8. Mocha Brownies

When preparing a tea tray, you can use any favourite cookie, bar or cupcake recipe. Remember to keep it small and dainty and try to provide a combination of shapes and colours to provide visual appeal.

TEMPEST SWEET SCONES

Before I opened the Tea Room, I experimented with dozens and dozens of scone recipes to find the perfect one. My requirement was that they be light and flakey, held their shape well after being baked (presentation is everything, after all), and were just a little bit sweet. After narrowing it down, I fiddled with the recipe some more, added my own twist, and came up with the perfect scone. I must say, this process took me the better part of a month. Initially, my family thought they'd died and gone to scone heaven, but toward the end, I swear I heard groans when I pulled the scones from the oven!

Scones are nicest served the day they are baked. If you must have them the next day, warm them slightly in the oven to crisp them up a bit. Ideally, scones are best with Devon cream and jam or preserves. Devon cream is available at select grocery stores, but is very expensive. If you are unable to find Devon cream, you can certainly use sweetened whipped cream or lemon curd.

6 cups flour
¾ cup granulated sugar
3 tbsp baking powder
1½ tsp salt
¾ cup cold shortening, cut in ½ inch cubes
¾ cup cold unsalted butter, cut into ½ inch cubes
2 ¼ cups milk
Grated zest of 2 lemons
½ cup currants
Milk, coarse sugar

Preheat oven to 400ºF.
- In a large bowl, combine flour, sugar, baking powder and salt.
- Using pastry blender or two knives, cut in shortening and butter until crumbly, the pieces roughly the size of peas.
- Add lemon zest and currants; stir with wooden spoon.
- Add milk all at once; stir with fork to make a soft sticky dough.
- Turn dough out onto lightly floured surface; knead about 12 times, with a light hand. Overworking this dough will result in a tough, heavy scone.
- Gently pat out dough into a 1 inch thick disc.
- Using a 2 ½ inch cookie cutter cut out scones, re-rolling scraps.
- Brush scones with milk; then sprinkle with coarse sugar.

- Bake for 16 – 18 minutes, until lightly golden.

Makes about 25 scones.

Alternatively, you can divide the dough into three equal discs and slice the discs into 6 portions each. This will give you slightly larger, pie shaped scones. Adjust the baking time; they will require a few more minutes to bake. Makes 18 scones.

Variations: Instead of lemon and currants, try any of the following: orange zest and cranberries, sweet dried cherries and almond slivers, candied ginger and lemon zest, or mini chocolate chips.

These scones freeze beautifully. Freeze the <u>unbaked</u> scones individually on a baking sheet. When frozen solid, store in plastic freezer bags. Bake a couple at a time as needed. When baking from frozen, add about 5 minutes to the baking time, remembering to watch them closely.

*A note about baking times:

As ovens vary, please watch your scones carefully, checking them a few minutes before the suggested time.

LEMON CURD

This curd can be prepared several days in advance and stored in the refrigerator; use any extra as a spread for your morning toast.

3 large egg yolks
Zest of ½ a lemon
¼ cup freshly squeezed lemon juice (about 2 lemons)
6 tbsp sugar
4 tbsp unsalted butter, cold and cut into ½ inch pieces

- Combine yolks, lemon zest, lemon juice, and sugar in a small saucepan. Whisk to combine.
- Set over medium heat and stir constantly with a wooden spoon, making sure to stir sides and bottom of pan. Stir until mixture is thick enough to coat back of wooden spoon, 5 to 7 minutes.
- Remove saucepan from heat. Add butter, one piece at a time, stirring with the wooden spoon until smooth.
- Transfer mixture to a medium bowl. Lay a sheet of plastic wrap directly on surface of the curd to avoid a skin from forming; wrap tightly.
- Let cool; refrigerate until firm and chilled, at least one hour. Store for two days.

SHORTBREAD

In its simplest form, shortbread is a concoction of three main ingredients: flour, butter and sugar. These are the mother of all butter cookies and are enjoyed year round throughout the world, but more commonly consumed at Christmas.

To make the best shortbread always, always use real butter. Nothing else will do. In the Tea Room, we used two varieties of shortbread. A cookie shaped in a teapot which we served with our cream teas and afternoon teas, or the traditional Petticoat Tails which are baked in a circle and cut into wedges. The recipes for both follow:

TEAPOT SHORTBREAD

2 cups unsalted butter, at room temperature
1 cup granulated sugar
4 cups all purpose flour

Preheat oven to 350ºF.
- Cream butter; add sugar gradually.
- Add flour, making sure it is well mixed, but don't overwork.
- Roll out dough on a lightly floured surface to a ¼ inch thickness.
- Using a 2 inch cookie cutter (any shape you choose) cut out and place on an ungreased cookie sheet.
- Bake 13 – 15* minutes until cookies are a light golden colour.

*Because of the high butter content, these cookies brown quickly. I recommend baking a small batch first. If they brown too quickly, drop the temperature to 325º or shorten the baking time on the next batch.

Variation: If using a round or heart shaped cookie cutter, dip ½ the cooled cookie in melted chocolate for a great taste sensation.

Makes about 4 dozen cookies.

PETTICOAT TAILS

This is a lovely Scottish shortbread recipe. The addition of the lemon or orange rind really pumps up the flavour.

2 cups all purpose flour
½ tsp baking powder
1cup unsalted butter, at room temperature
½ cup granulated sugar
1 tbsp grated lemon or orange rind

Preheat oven to 300ºF.
* Sift together the flour and baking powder.
* Cream the butter until light and fluffy; add sugar gradually and continue beating until well blended.
* Add the flour, baking powder mixture; add rind; mixing until dough comes together. Do not overwork.
* Pat the dough into a greased 9 inch glass pie plate.
* With a knife carefully cut the dough in 16 pie shaped wedges.
* Prick the shortbread with the tunes of a fork; then press around the diameter of the plate with the fork to get a ruffled edge.
* Bake for about 33 - 40 minutes or until lightly golden.

The edges will run together during baking, so retrace the original knife marks while the shortbread is still warm. Cool completely.

EMPIRE COOKIES

Old fashioned and dainty, these delicious filled and iced sugar cookies are perfect for the tea tray.

2/3 cup butter, at room temperature
½ cup granulated sugar
1 egg
1 tsp vanilla
2 cups all purpose flour
1 tsp baking powder
Pinch salt
1/3 cup raspberry jam, approx

Icing:
1 cup icing sugar
1/8 tsp almond extract
1 tbsp hot water, approx
6 candied cherries

Preheat oven to 350°F.
- In bowl, cream butter and sugar until fluffy.
- Beat in egg and vanilla.
- In separate bowl, stir together flour, baking powder and salt.
- Gradually stir flour mixture into butter mixture.
- Between two sheets of waxed paper, roll dough to 1/8 inch thickness.
- Using a two inch cookie cutter, cut rounds; transfer to lightly greased cookie sheets.
- Bake for 8 – 10 minutes or until very lightly browned. Let cool completely.
- Spread half the cookies with a thin layer of raspberry jam; top with remaining cookies
- To make the icing, combine icing sugar and almond extract in a bowl. Stir in enough hot water to make icing spreadable.
- Ice cookie tops. Slice cherries into slivers; top each cookie with sliver

Makes about 30 cookies.

OLD FASHIONED LEMON TARTS

Basic Pastry Dough

1 ¼ cups all purpose flour
1 tbsp sugar
½ tsp salt
¼ cup cold unsalted butter, cut into ¾ inch pieces
3 tbsp cold vegetable shortening, cut in ¾ inch pieces
3 tbsp ice water

• Place flour, sugar and salt in the bowl of a food processor. Pulse to blend.
• Add the pieces of butter and shortening and pulse until reduced to ½ inch pieces
• Add water a little at a time and pulse until the dough just begins to come together in a rough mass.
• Shape dough into a 5 inch disk and wrap in plastic film; refrigerate for about two hours.
• Remove from fridge, and let sit for 5 minutes.
• Roll dough out on lightly floured surface to a 1/8 inch thickness.
• Cut the dough out using a cookie cutter ½ inch larger than the size of your tart pans.
• Refrigerate dough in tart pans until your filling is ready.

Lemon Tart Filling

Preheat oven to 350°F.

1 lemon
4 eggs
2 cups granulated sugar
½ cup butter
16 tart shells, approx. 2 ½ inch

• Cut lemons in quarters, then thinly slice; remove seeds
• Place in blender or food processor along with eggs, sugar and butter; process until lemon is finely chopped.
• Divide mixture evenly among chilled tart shells.
• Place tart pans on baking sheet and bake for 20 – 25 minutes or until lightly browned.

Makes about 16 small tarts.

MADELEINES

These shell shaped French cookies are cake-like in texture and are a traditional tea-time treat in France.

Madeleine pans are available at specialty kitchen supply stores.

¼ cup unsalted butter, more to brush on pans
1 tbsp honey
1 tsp vanilla extract
¾ cup all purpose flour
1 tsp baking powder
¾ tsp ground cardamom
1 tsp finely grated orange zest
¼ tsp salt
¼ cup granulated sugar
2 large eggs

Preheat oven to 325ºF.
• Brush pans with melted butter and set aside.
• Melt ¼ cup butter in small saucepan over low heat. Remove from heat and stir in honey and vanilla. Let cool 10 minutes.
• Mix flour, baking powder, cardamom, orange zest and salt in a small bowl. Set aside.
• In bowl of mixer, mix together eggs and sugar until light and creamy. By hand, gently fold in flour mixture until well combined.
• Add butter mixture and continue to fold until combined.
• Cover with wrap and refrigerate for 30 minutes.
• Spoon batter into prepared pans, filling only halfway. Tap pan on work surface to eliminate air bubbles.
• Bake until cookies are puffed and lightly golden, about 7 – 8 minutes.
• Let cool slightly; unmold onto wire cooling rack. Let cool completely
• Dust with icing sugar.

Makes 16 madeleines.

MINI LEMON COCONUT CUPCAKES

Snow topped with a tangy cream cheese icing, these cupcakes freeze well.

½ cup unsalted butter, softened
1 cup granulated sugar
2 eggs
1 ½ cups all purpose flour
½ cup shredded sweetened coconut
4 tsp grated lemon rind
1 tsp baking powder
¼ tsp salt
½ cup milk

Lemon Cream Cheese Icing:
2 tbsp cream cheese, softened
1 tbsp unsalted butter, softened
½ tsp grated lemon rind
1 ½ tsp lemon juice
1 cup icing sugar
½ cup shredded sweetened coconut

Preheat oven to 350ºF.
•   In bowl, beat butter with sugar until light, beat in eggs, one at a time; beating after each addition.
•   In separate bowl, whisk flour, coconut, lemon rind, baking powder and salt; stir into butter mixture alternately with milk, making 3 additions of dry ingredients and 2 of milk.
•   Spoon into 24 paper lined mini muffin cups.
•   Bake in centre of oven for 12 – 14 minutes or until tester inserted in centre come out clean. Remove from pan to rack; let cool completely.

Lemon Cream Cheese Icing:
•   In bowl, beat cream cheese and butter until combined; add lemon rind, juice and mix well.
•   Gradually add icing sugar until well combined and spreadable. If too thick, add more lemon juice.
•   Spread over cupcakes and top with shredded coconut.

Makes 24 mini cupcakes.

MOCHA BROWNIES

These dense brownies are always a treat. For a pretty presentation, cut diagonally into diamond shapes and dust ½ of each diamond with icing sugar.

½ cup butter
2 oz unsweetened chocolate, coarsely chopped
½ cup semi sweet chocolate chips
1 tbsp instant coffee granules
2 eggs
1 cup granulated sugar
1 ½ tsp vanilla
Pinch salt
½ cup all purpose flour

Preheat oven to 350°F.
• In bowl over saucepan of hot (not boiling) water, heat together butter, unsweetened chocolate, chocolate chips and coffee granules until nearly all chocolate is melted.
• Remove from heat; stir until smooth.
• In separate bowl, beat eggs with sugar until pale and thickened; stir in chocolate mixture, vanilla and salt. Fold in flour.
• Spread in greased 8 inch square pan and bake in oven for 20 – 25 minutes or until edges pull slightly away from pan and cake tester inserted in centre comes out with a few moist crumbs.
• Let cool on rack; cut into squares or diamonds.

Makes about 12 brownies

Chapter Four
Reminiscence
Soups and Savoury Scones

Marie rinsed her hands under the hot running water, lathering up with the sweet smelling citrus soap to chase away the last bits of soil underneath her fingernails. She had had a productive morning tidying up first the house and then the garden, but now was feeling the first stirrings of hunger. She dried her hands on the tea towel by the stove; then carefully replaced it on the oven door handle. Marie glanced at the big clock on the wall and was surprised at the time. How slowly the minutes were going by! Surely, it should be lunch time by now! She had made arrangements to meet her friend Arlene for lunch today, and though they often met for lunch, this day Marie felt the jitteriness of anticipation. She was at a loss to explain just why she felt this anticipation – it was just an ordinary lunch date, one of several they made together during the week. They were meeting at the Tempest today, as they often did, and Marie decided that it was the combination of seeing her good friend at their favourite spot, and the expectation of her favourite soup that had her giddy today. She looked at the clock again, and decided she would go a bit early and wait for Arlene at the tea room – "Oh no!" she thought to herself. "I forgot to call and make reservations!" The calmness of the morning was suddenly replaced with agitation. She was annoyed with herself. How could she forget? The last thing she remembered saying to Arlene was that she would take care of the reservations. The tea room was fairly small, with only a 20 seat capacity, so it sometimes filled up quite quickly, as she and Arlene had found out one time too many. "Oh, why was it everyone in town wanted to eat at the exact same time?" Marie muttered to herself as she reached for the telephone. Hopefully she wasn't too late.

"Good morning, Marie," greeted Sara, the owner of the tea room. At first, Marie was impressed that Sara had recognized her voice with just a hello, but on consideration she thought it more likely she had call display service on her telephone. Marie knew that the sometimes frazzled owner of the tea room often struggled to remember all her customer's name, and when they first started frequenting the place on a regular basis, Sara had taken pains to write her and Arlene's names, along with a brief description, in the back of a small notebook she kept in a drawer by the cash register. She explained to the two women that it helped twig her cluttered memory. Both she and Arlene had been amused by that…she wasn't even that old, but Sara often claimed that she had a memory like a sieve and operating a business and having two teenage sons was reason enough to resort to memory aids. One day, Arlene had curiously asked Sara what description she had put alongside their names and the owner had beamed them a big smile and said, "Why, the soup ladies, of course!"

Marie and Arlene met regularly for lunch at the Tempest, sometimes as often as two or three times a week. It was a good place to eat. The food was great, the prices were reasonable and it felt just like home. The service, too, was exceptional; they were often in and out in under an hour so that Arlene could get back to work on time. Sara had told them they were two of her easiest and most delightful customers. She always made an effort to spend a few minutes with them when they came in, often to discuss their mutually favourite TV show, *Dancing with the Stars*. They had spent many weeks debating the merits of the various dancers, or commiserating over the elimination of their favourite couple. The two ladies were such a regular feature in the tea room, that the staff had affectionately dubbed them 'the soup ladies' as they always ordered the same thing. In fact, they had no need to see the menu; two soups of the day, two savoury scones and two waters. Occasionally, they might be tempted to order dessert; especially it was any kind of crisp, crumble or pie.

"Can you accommodate us today?" asked Marie, hopefully.

"Certainly can," answered the owner. "Coming at 12:00?"

"Yes, just after twelve, if that's okay?" asked Marie with a smile. "By the way, what's the soup today?" She hoped it would be one of her favourites, though in truth it would be difficult to know just which one she liked the best…sweet potato pear, squash and apple, roasted carrot. All of these were equally delicious especially when accompanied with a freshly baked savoury scone, oozing with cheddar and speckled with fresh chives.

"Why, your favourite, of course!" laughed Sara.

Marie chuckled as she hung up. That was the standing joke between them; all the soups were her favourite! Yes, life was definitely good, she thought to herself as she walked up the stairs to change. Good friends, good food, what more can one ask for?

Back at the tea room, Sara jotted their names down in the reservation book. She so looked forward to seeing this merry pair that always had a smile on their freckled faces and a giggle on their lips. To see them come into the store was like sunshine on a rainy day. No matter how busy or frazzled she was, the 'soup ladies' always managed to lighten the mood. Today, she was certain they would order the apple cranberry crisp. Sara walked toward the kitchen to reserve two desserts of the day for the soup ladies.

RECIPES

SOUPS AND SAVOURY SCONES

"There is nothing like soup. It is by nature eccentric: no two are ever alike, unless of course you get your soup in a can."

Laurie Colwin, Home Cooking

1. Savoury Scones with Cheddar and Chives

2. Sweet Potato and Pear Soup

3. Roasted Carrot Soup

4. Broccoli and Cheddar Soup

5. Cream of Asparagus Soup

6. Corn Chowder

7. Pumpkin and Apple Soup

8. Beef Barley Soup

9. Tomato Fennel Soup

10. Leek and Potato Soup

SAVOURY SCONES

These scones are light and flakey and a real treat warm from the oven with a pat of fresh butter. They are even better when enjoyed with a steamy bowl of soup on a cold winter day. Our customers often ordered them frozen to bake up at home.

Although chives are called for in this recipe, feel free to experiment with other fresh herbs.

4 cups flour
2 tbsp baking powder
2 tsp salt
½ cup cold unsalted butter, cut into ½ inch cubes
½ cup cold shortening
1½ cups buttermilk
1 cup shredded sharp cheddar
½ cup chopped fresh chives

1 egg mixed with 1 tbsp water for egg wash

Preheat oven to 400°F.
- In a large bowl, combine flour, baking powder and salt.
- Using pastry blender or two knives; cut in shortening and butter until crumbly.
- Add buttermilk; stir with fork to make a soft, sticky dough
- Add fresh herbs and cheddar cheese and mix until just combined.
- Turn dough out onto lightly floured surface; knead lightly, about 12 times.
- Gently pat out dough into a 1 inch thick disc.
- Using a 2 ½ inch cookie cutter; cut out scones, re-rolling scraps.
- Brush scones with egg wash.
- Bake for about 20- 22 minutes or until lightly golden.

Makes about 18 scones.

Like the sweet scones, you can individually freeze these and bake from frozen. Adjust baking time. They are best enjoyed the day they are baked.

SWEET POTATO AND PEAR SOUP

A great soup for warming up the winter; it has a touch of sweetness and a hint of heat. Although easy to make for a casual family night dinner, it's also a sophisticated choice for company. It was one of our most requested soups.

1 tbsp butter
1 small onion, chopped
¼ cup chopped carrot
¼ cup chopped celery
3 medium sweet potatoes, peeled and diced
1 pear, peeled and diced
2 tsp fresh thyme leaves, or ½ tsp dried thyme
1 tsp paprika
5 cups chicken broth (low salt or home made)
1/3 cup whipping cream, optional
2 tsp maple syrup
2 tsp lime juice
Salt and freshly ground pepper

- In a large pot, melt butter. Add onion, carrot and celery and sauté for 1 minute. Add sweet potatoes, pear and thyme and sauté for about 2 minutes. Add paprika and chicken broth.
- Bring to a boil and simmer for 15 – 20 minutes or until sweet potato is soft.
- Puree in a blender or food processor until smooth. Return to pot.
- Add cream (if using), maple syrup and lime juice. Simmer for 5 minutes. If soup is too thick, add a little extra broth.
- Season with salt and pepper, as needed. Can be made up to two days ahead.

Makes 8 servings.

ROASTED CARROT SOUP

The cumin in this soup gives it a nicely exotic flavour, and roasting the carrots brings out a caramelized sweetness.

4 tsp butter, melted
½ tsp black pepper, divided
2 lbs carrots, cut into 2 inch pieces
Cooking spray
1½ cups water
2 tsp chopped fresh thyme, or ½ tsp dried thyme
1 tbsp butter
½ tsp ground cumin
1½ tbsp honey
1 tbsp fresh lime juice
2 – 900 ml boxes vegetable or chicken stock

Preheat oven to 400°F.
• Combine 4 tsp melted butter, ¼ tsp pepper and carrots in a shallow roasting pan coated with cooking spray; toss to coat. Bake for about 35 minutes or until tender, stirring every 10 minutes.
• In a food processor, puree roasted carrots with water and thyme; process until smooth.
• Melt 1 tbsp butter in a large saucepan over medium heat, add the cumin, and cook 30 seconds or until fragrant, stirring constantly.
• Add pureed carrot mixture, ¼ tsp pepper, honey, lime juice, and broth; bring to a simmer over medium heat.

Makes 7 servings.

BROCCOLI AND CHEDDAR SOUP

This soup has a smooth texture and mild flavour. It is thick and filling, and is a great way to get kids to eat their broccoli.

1 tbsp butter
1 cup chopped onion
2 garlic cloves, chopped
3 cups chicken broth, low sodium or home made
1 lb broccoli florets
2 ½ cups milk
1/3 cups all purpose flour
¼ tsp black pepper
2 cups shredded cheddar cheese

- In a large saucepan over medium high heat, melt butter and add onions and garlic; sauté 3 minutes or until tender.
- Add broth and broccoli. Bring mixture to a boil over medium-high heat. Reduce heat to medium, cook 15 – 20 minutes or until broccoli is cooked.
- In a cup, combine milk and flour, stirring with a whisk until well blended; add to broccoli mixture. Cook 5 minutes or until slightly thick, stirring constantly. Stir in pepper.
- Remove from heat; add cheese, stirring until melted.
- Place one-third of soup in a blender or food processor; process until smooth. Return pureed soup to pan.

Makes 6 servings.

CREAM OF ASPARAGUS SOUP

This is an easy soup to make and is dressy enough for a company dinner. Garnish with thin asparagus spears for an elegant presentation.

3 cups asparagus (about one lb), sliced in ½ inch pieces
2 cups chicken broth, low sodium or home made
¾ tsp chopped fresh thyme, divided
bay leaf
1 garlic clove, crushed
1 tbsp all purpose flour
2 cups milk
Dash of ground nutmeg
2 tsp butter
¾ tsp salt
¼ tsp grated lemon rind

• Combine asparagus, broth, ½ thyme, bay leaf, and crushed garlic in a large saucepan over medium-high heat; bring to a boil. Cover, reduce heat and simmer 10 minutes. Discard bay leaf.
• In batches, place asparagus mixture in a blender; cover tightly and process until smooth.
• Using a clean dry pan, place flour in pan. Gradually add milk, stirring with a whisk until blended. Add the pureed asparagus and ground nutmeg; stir to combine.
• Bring to a boil. Reduce heat; simmer 5 minutes, stirring constantly. Remove from heat, and stir in remaining ¼ tsp thyme, butter, salt and lemon rind.

Makes 4 servings.

CORN CHOWDER

Chowders are always hearty, and this one is no exception. The bacon adds a nice smokiness to the soup.

5 slices bacon, cut into ¼ inch pieces
2 tbsp butter
2 cups chopped onion
2 tbsp all purpose flour
4 cups chicken or vegetable stock, low salt
2 large white potatoes, peeled and cut into ½ dice
1 cup light cream
¾ tsp white pepper, or to taste
4 cups fresh or frozen corn kernels
1 large red pepper, cut into ½ inch dice
3 green onions, chopped
1 tbsp chopped fresh cilantro for garnish, optional

- Cook bacon in a large stockpot over low heat until fat is rendered, about 5 minutes.
- Add butter to pot and melt; then add the onion, and cook for about 10 minutes, or until soft but not browned. Spoon in the flour and cook, stirring for another 2 – 3 minutes.
- Add stock with the potatoes. Continue cooking over medium-low heat until potatoes and just tender, 10 – 15 minutes.
- Add the cream, white pepper and salt and cook for about 3 minutes.
- Toss in the corn, red pepper, and green onions and adjust seasonings if necessary. Cook for another 5 – 10 minutes. Serve immediately and garnish with cilantro, if using.

Makes 6 – 8 servings.

BEEF AND BARLEY SOUP

This is a wonderfully warming winter soup. Rich and nutritious, its heartiness made it a favourite with our male customers.

Cooking spray
2 lbs beef stew meat, trimmed and cut into 1 inch pieces
2 tsp canola oil
2 cups chopped leek, about 4 medium
2 cups chopped carrot
4 cloves garlic, minced
6 cups water
1½ tsp salt
2 tsp fresh thyme leaves, or 1 tsp dried
½ tsp black pepper
4 bay leaves
2 – 900 ml boxes beef broth
1 cup uncooked pearl barley.

• Heat a large stock pot over medium-high heat. Coat pan with cooking spray. Add half of beef; cook 5 minutes, browning on all sides. Remove from pan. Repeat procedure with remaining beef.
• In same pan, heat oil over medium-high heat. Add leek, carrot, and garlic, sauté 4 minutes or until lightly browned. Return beef to pan. Add water and next 5 ingredients (through broth); bring to a boil. Cover, reduce heat and simmer one hour.
• Add barley; cook 30 minutes or until beef and barley are tender. Discard bay leaves.

Makes about 8 servings.

PUMPKIN AND APPLE SOUP

You can use Granny Smith apples instead of the Spys. We mostly used butternut squash for this recipe, but pumpkin is just as nice.

¼ cup butter
3 cups chopped onion
6 cups chopped pumpkin or butternut squash
2 Spy apples, peeled and chopped
1 tsp brown sugar
Pinch of cinnamon
Pinch of allspice
Small pinch of cayenne
1 tsp salt
5 cups chicken or vegetable stock
Salt and freshly ground pepper

•   In a large pot, melt butter over medium heat. Add onion and cook until softened, about 3 minutes.
•   Add the pumpkin (or squash) and apples and cook until softened, another 3 minutes. Add the brown sugar and spices; then chicken or vegetable stock and simmer for 30 minutes.
•   Remove from heat, blend until smooth with a hand blender or in a food processor. Season to taste with salt and pepper.

Makes 6 – 8 servings.

FENNEL AND TOMATO SOUP

This is a European variation on a tomato soup. The ginger gives it an exotic touch.

2 medium bulbs fennel
1 large onion, diced
1 clove garlic, minced
2 tbsp olive oil
2 tsp finely diced fresh ginger
1 tsp ground fennel
½ tsp dried chili flakes
2 cups chicken stock, low sodium or home made
3 tbsp tomato paste
1-28 ounce (796 ml) can diced tomatoes
Salt and pepper to taste

• Trim any discoloured or damaged leaves from fennel bulbs. Cut off and reserve springs for garnish. Quarter bulbs, discarding wood cores. Dice fennel and set aside. Yield about 4 cups.
• In a large saucepan, over medium heat, sauté onion, garlic and ginger in olive oil until onion begins to soften but has not browned. Add fennel and sauté, stirring frequently, for 5 minutes or until fennel begins to soften. Add spices, chicken stock, and tomato paste and diced tomatoes.
• Reduce heat, cooking on low boil, uncovered for about 15 – 20 minutes or until fennel is tender crisp. Do not overcook. Garnish with reserved fennel.

Makes 6 servings.

LEEK AND POTATO SOUP

One of the tea room's most requested soups; this can be served hot or cold.

3 tbsp vegetable oil
2 leeks, white and pale green parts only, thinly sliced
1 each, celery and carrot, diced
¼ tsp salt
1 tsp fresh thyme leaves, or ¼ tsp dried
¼ tsp white pepper or black pepper
2 large Yukon Gold potatoes, peeled and chopped
6 cups low sodium chicken stock, or home made
Fresh chives, chopped

- In large pot, heat oil over medium-high heat; sauté leeks, celery, carrot, salt, thyme and pepper until softened, about 8 minutes.
- Add potatoes, and stock; bring to a boil. Reduce heat, cover and simmer until potatoes are tender, about 20 minutes.
- Using a hand blender, or in a regular blender, in batches, puree soup until smooth.
- Serve garnished with chopped chives.

Makes 4 – 6 servings.

Chapter Five
Reminiscence
Quiche

Kathleen was completely out of sorts today. The bad news she received several days ago from her dearest friend was breaking her heart. She could not shake this lethargy that had taken hold of her. It did not help that she had barely slept last night. Life was just not fair, she thought to herself. But then she had always known that, always accepted it for what it was, always forged on with her usual sense of good humour and bluntness that were her trademark. She would write the eulogy that she knew would soon be needed for her life-long friend in the same way she had always approached anything – sail up and full steam ahead. She was sure her friend would not want it any other way.

She heaved herself out of her chair with a heaviness of limb she had not noticed before and made some phone calls. Shortly afterward, with her hat pulled firmly over her short hair, no trace of make-up on her lined, 75 year old face, she found herself making her way to the tea room. A nice bracing cup of tea, that was what she needed right now. She supposed she could always make one up for herself at home, but it was not the same, and she hadn't the energy.

As she stepped inside the tea room, she couldn't help but notice how the grey, damp day seemed to mirror her own somber mood. It was late in the afternoon and the place was nearly empty. It was such a lovely space, the tea room. A short walk through the gift shoppe, and under the ivy topped cedar arbour, led you to an intimate area that was both cozy and elegant. When it had first opened, Kathleen had been captivated by the quotes that were hand painted on the walls. They all related to tea. Her eyes were drawn now to her favourite quote, *"Strange how the teapot can represent at the same time, the comfort of solitude and the pleasure of company."* Today she would enjoy her tea in solitude, but her mind went back to the many occasions when she had sat here with her dear friend and their red hat sisters and had had wonderful, fun times, full of laughter and joy. One particularly joyful occasion came to mind. She and several of her red hat sisters had made arrangements to meet for lunch at the tea room. They had sat agonizing for some time over the menu, each of them extolling their favourite sandwich, and debating as to why their choice was the best thing on the menu. Soon, a server brought out two slices of quiche to the adjacent table, and Kathleen and her friends listened as the ladies next to them ooh-ed and aah-ed over the crisp, tender crust and the mouth watering flavour of the sun dried tomato and feta quiche. They claimed it was the best quiche they had had. Soon, everyone at Kathleen's table quickly changed their minds and they all ordered the quiche. The memory brought a teary smile to Kathleen's face.

She sat herself down at a table for four in the corner. She knew that occupying a table so large for just one person would normally be frowned upon, but it was highly unlikely to get much busier at this time of day, and there was no reservation sign on the table. Today, she had need of space around her. Even though there was only one other table occupied, she did not want to sit too close to happy people today. She ordered her favourite tea, and contemplated how strange life was. While she sat here full of sadness and reflecting on a decades old friendship, the two women who sat across the room were full of animation and laughter. She sipped her Cream of Earl Grey tea, enjoying its rich smoothness, and surreptitiously listened to the friends' conversation. It was evident that they were 'catching up' and hadn't seen each other in awhile, as they passed photographers across the table, one to the other, in a flurry of animation. *You're a grandmother now! How many grandchildren? Italy? No, we usually go to the Caribbean. You're doing what? Teaching bellydancing? I don't believe it!*

Kathleen secretly smiled at the conversation she shouldn't have been minding, and was suddenly feeling much better, happier, if one could use the term. Well, maybe not happy, but calmer and resigned. Whatever life threw at you, Kathleen was a firm believer in getting on with it. Today she was sad; she was soon to loose a dear friend, but she knew that tomorrow was full of new possibilities. She was surrounded by a richness of friends and family that would gather round her and support her, and make her laugh again. Her eyes strayed to another anonymous quote on the wall, *"Life is a cup to be filled, not drained."* Very appropriate, thought Kathleen as she enjoyed her tea.

RECIPES
QUICHE

"Bring back the quiche."

Julia Child

1. Classic pastry dough for quiche

2. Quiche Lorraine

3. Spinach Feta Quiche

4. Sun dried Tomato and Feta Cheese Quiche

5. Broccoli Cheddar Quiche

6. Salmon and Dill Quiche

7. Roasted Red Pepper and Artichoke Quiche

PASTRY FOR QUICHE

In the Tea Room we made up enough pastry every Tuesday to last us the week using a large quantity recipe that is not easy to divide up. So for ease of preparation I've given you a similar recipe that I've had good results with. This recipe produces two crusts for a 9 inch pie plate. Tuck the other in the freezer if you are not using it right away. Freeze the unbaked pastry dough already rolled out in the quiche dish or pie plate, then blind bake from the frozen state, remembering to add about 5 minutes baking time. When you have one tucked away in the freezer, you can put together a quiche for supper in no time at all.

2 cups all purpose flour
1 cup cold shortening
¾ tsp salt
1 egg
2 tbsp ice water
1 tbsp white vinegar

Preheat oven to 400° F.

• Combine flour and salt and mix to incorporate. With a pastry blender or two knives, cut cold shortening into flour mixture (or pulse in a food processor) just until crumbly, the pieces roughly the size of peas.
• Whisk ice water, egg and vinegar together to blend. Pour all of the liquid evenly over the flour mixture. Stir with a fork until all the mixture is moistened (or pulse in processor) until incorporated. Squeeze a small handful; if it doesn't hold together, add ½ tbsp more ice water at a time, stirring until just incorporated. Do not overwork mixture or pastry will be tough.
• Divide dough in half and shape into a ball. Flatten slightly and cover in plastic wrap. Chill in refrigerator for 30 minutes.
• Dust rolling pin and work surface lightly with flour. Roll out the pastry until it is about 1 ½ inches larger than your 9 inch pie plate.
• To transfer pastry easily, drape loosely over rolling pin and place carefully into pie plate without stretching. Prick the base of pastry with fork. Refrigerate for 30 minutes.

To blind bake:
• Line chilled or frozen pastry (in pie plate) with foil and fill with pie weights or dried beans.

- Bake for 20 – 25 minutes, then remove the beans and the foil and bake for another 5 minutes.

Makes pastry for two quiches.

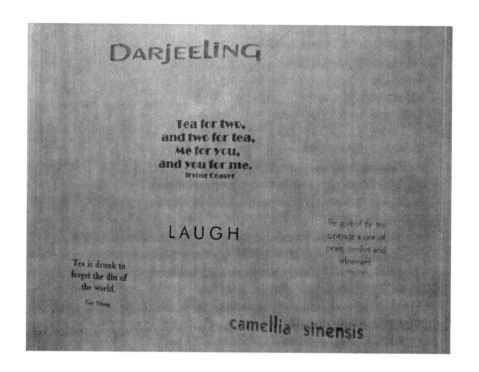

QUICHE LORRAINE

This is the quiche that started it all! Though a very basic, simple recipe, it is always a popular one.

Pastry for one quiche, already blind baked
1 tbsp butter
12 slices bacon
4 eggs
1¾ cups whipping cream
¾ tsp salt
1/8 tsp ground nutmeg
1 cup shredded Swiss cheese

Preheat oven to 425º F.
- In a large skillet, over medium heat, fry bacon slices until crisp and brown. Drain onto paper towels to remove excess grease.
- Sprinkle shredded Swiss cheese onto prepared piecrust. Crumble bacon slices over top.
- In a bowl, with wire whisk, beat eggs, cream, salt and nutmeg.
- Pour egg mixture over top of cheese and bacon on piecrust. Bake for 15 minutes at 425º, then lower oven temperature to 325º; bake for an additional 25 minutes or until top is golden.
- Quiche is cooked when knife inserted in centre comes out clean. Let cool 10 minutes before serving.

Makes 6 servings.

SPINACH FETA QUICHE

Also known as Quiche Florentine, it is a classic.

Pastry for one quiche, already blind baked
1 tbsp vegetable oil
½ large onion, chopped finely
1 clove garlic, minced
1 - 300 gram package frozen chopped spinach, squeezed dry
1 cup shredded Swiss cheese
½ cup feta cheese, crumbled

4 eggs
¾ cup milk
¾ cup whipping cream
½ tsp salt
¼ tsp black pepper
1/8 tsp nutmeg

Preheat oven to 375° F.
• In a medium skillet, in 1 tbsp oil, cook onion and garlic until soft. Add spinach and cook for 3 minutes. Remove from heat.
• In medium bowl, whisk eggs, milk, cream, salt, pepper and nutmeg until well combined.
• Place shredded Swiss cheese in prepared piecrust; top with spinach and onion mixture. Sprinkle ½ cup crumbled feta cheese over top; pour in egg mixture.
• Bake in centre of oven for about 40 – 45 minutes, or until centre is set. Quiche is cooked when knife inserted in centre comes out clean.

Makes 6 servings.

SUN DRIED TOMATO AND FETA QUICHE

The robust flavour of the sun dried tomatoes marries well with the feta cheese.

Pastry for one quiche, already blind baked
1 tbsp vegetable oil
½ large onion, chopped finely
1 clove garlic, minced
1/3 cup chopped sun dried tomatoes; packed in oil; excess oil drained
1 cup shredded Swiss cheese
½ cup feta cheese, crumbled

4 eggs
¾ cup milk
¾ up whipping cream
½ tsp salt
¼ tsp black pepper
1 tsp fresh thymes leaves, or ¼ tsp dried

Preheat oven to 375º F.
•   In a medium skillet, in 1 tbsp oil, cook onion and garlic until soft. Add sun dried tomatoes and cook for 3 minutes. Remove from heat.
•   In medium bowl, whisk eggs, milk, cream, salt, pepper and fresh thyme until well combined.
•   Place shredded Swiss cheese in prepared piecrust; top with sun dried tomatoes and onion mixture. Sprinkle ½ cup crumbled feta cheese over top; pour in egg mixture.
•   Bake in centre of oven for about 40 – 45 minutes, or until centre is set. Quiche is cooked when knife inserted in centre comes out clean.

Makes 6 servings.

BROCCOLI CHEDDAR QUICHE

There is something very complementary about broccoli and cheddar together, whether in a soup or a quiche.

Pastry for one quiche, already blind baked
1 tbsp vegetable oil
½ large onion, chopped finely
1 clove garlic, minced
1 300 gram package frozen chopped broccoli
1½ cups shredded cheddar cheese

4 eggs
¾ cup milk
¾ cup whipping cream
½ tsp salt
¼ tsp black pepper

Preheat oven to 375° F.

• In a medium skillet, in 1 tbsp oil, cook onion and garlic until soft. Add frozen broccoli and cook for 3 minutes. Remove from heat.

• In medium bowl, whisk eggs, milk, cream, salt, pepper until well combined.

• Place shredded cheddar cheese in prepared piecrust; top with broccoli and onion mixture. Pour egg mixture over top.

• Bake in centre of oven for about 40 – 45 minutes, or until centre is set. Quiche is cooked when knife inserted in centre comes out clean.

Makes 6 servings.

SALMON AND DILL QUICHE

This is one of my personal favourites. The smokiness of the salmon, the smoothness of the creamy cheese and the addition of the capers all combine to make it truly special. Enjoy this with a cup of Lapsang Souchong tea.

Pastry for one quiche, already blind baked
1 tbsp vegetable oil
2 leeks, white and pale green part only, chopped finely
50 grams smoked salmon, torn in small pieces
125 grams cream cheese, cut in ½ cubes
2 tbsp chopped fresh dill
1 tbsp capers

4 eggs
¾ cup milk
¾ cup whipping cream
½ tsp salt
¼ tsp black pepper
1 tbsp Dijon mustard

Preheat oven to 375° F.
- In a medium skillet, in 1 tbsp oil, cook leek until soft. Remove from heat.
- Sprinkle leek into prepared piecrust. Shred smoked salmon over top leeks; add cubed cream cheese. Sprinkle fresh dill and capers over salmon and cheese.
- In medium bowl, whisk eggs, milk, cream, salt, pepper and Dijon mustard until well combined. Pour egg mixture over top.
- Bake in centre of oven for about 40 – 45 minutes, or until centre is set. Quiche is cooked when knife inserted in centre comes out clean.

Makes 6 servings.

ROASTED RED PEPPER, ARTICHOKE AND ASIAGO CHEESE QUICHE

When we first introduced this quiche to the menu, it took a while for our customers to get past the artichoke (why does artichoke scare so many?) but after some time, they began to request it.

Pastry for one quiche, already blind baked
1 tbsp vegetable oil
½ large onion, chopped finely
1 clove garlic, minced
1/3 cup jarred roasted red peppers*, drained and chopped
1 - 6 oz can artichoke hearts, drained and chopped
1 cup shredded swiss cheese

4 eggs
¾ cup milk
¾ cup whipping cream
½ cup grated asiago or parmesan cheese
½ tsp salt
¼ tsp black pepper

Preheat oven to 375ºF.
• In a medium skillet, in 1 tbsp oil, cook onion and garlic until soft. Remove from heat and cool slightly.
• In prepared piecrust, add onion and garlic mixture and shredded Swiss cheese, then top with roasted red pepper and artichokes
• In medium bowl, whisk eggs, milk, cream, grated asiago or parmesan cheese, salt, and pepper until well combined. Pour over piecrust.
• Bake in centre of oven for about 40 – 45 minutes, or until centre is set. Quiche is cooked when knife inserted in centre comes out clean.

Makes 6 servings.

* When buying roasted red peppers in jars or cans, make sure they are not canned in a vinegar solution. If they are, rinse off and pat dry with paper towels before using, otherwise your quiche will taste of vinegar.

Chapter Six
Reminiscence
Sandwiches

Louise was struck by a jolt of cold, arctic air as she left her house on a clear frigid January day. Although she knew it was one of the coldest winters on record (the news and weather stations were talking of little else), Louise could not get used to the affront that met her each time she ventured out. Though the sun was high and brilliant in the sky, and she was dressed in hat, scarf, gloves and three layers of warm clothing, she could still feel the ice cold penetrating every fibre of her being. She quickly walked to the garage, her warm breath creating a white puff and her every footfall crunching on the freshly fallen snow. Louise was always amazed at the sheer contradiction of winter, so beautiful and pristine; and yet so brutally, unforgivingly cold.

Had it been an ordinary day, she would have certainly stayed in with one of her favourite books, snug and cozy in the warmth of her home, but today was no ordinary day and she wouldn't let the cold stop her.

She buckled herself into her car and turned the ignition, the motor reluctantly sputtering to life. It too, seemed to protest the cold. She debated going back into the house and letting the car warm up properly, but she did not relish the blast of wind she knew would be waiting for her once she left the car. No, she would wait it out and use to time to calm her mind and practice her smile. "Come on, Louise," she told herself, "Loosen your jaw; relax the muscles in your face." There, she could do it. Breathe and smile, smile and breathe. Louise could not help but feel a sense of both pride and panic arising within her. She was meeting her daughter Lyndsay for a late lunch at the tea room. They were regulars at the Tempest, and had been enjoying it there, either together or with their own varied friends, for the better part of five years. It was always fun to go there, and Louise knew that in many ways today would be no different, and yet….She felt her throat constricting as she thought of her only child departing this very day for the depths of Africa.

She thought about Lyndsay and all her accomplishments. What a lovely girl she had grown into. Her soft brown hair, delicate features and petite frame certainly set her apart from many girls her age, but it was her gentle heart that made her truly captivating. It was her gentle heart as well as her adventurous spirit that prompted her to Africa, a combination of both volunteer work and sight-seeing. Louise had sensed a restlessness in her daughter for some time now. She had trained and completed a number of marathons in the past few years including the grueling Ironman Triathalon. The exhausting and time consuming training had been her focus for so long that when Lyndsay had announced she would take a break from marathons this year, Louise had been somewhat surprised. She had wondered whether Lyndsay would grow bored without a major challenge on the horizon. For this reason, Louise knew that Lyndsay must take this voyage, though a very small and selfish part of her sometimes wished her daughter weren't quite so adventurous. Aside from worrying about her physical safety, she knew that she would miss her daughter so terribly much in the next three months. For Lyndsay was much more than just her daughter, she was also one of her dearest friends.

Lyndsay herself was very excited about her trip. She had wanted to go to Africa since she was a child. When she was younger, she thought it was nothing more than any other childhood fantasy, like wanting curly hair, or wanting to live in a tree house – something she knew deep down that would probably never happen. But the last few years, Lyndsay had begun to realize that it was within her reach to make it happen. When her church unexpectedly announced they would help finance her trip, she knew she couldn't pass it up. She spent weeks planning her itinerary, contacting host families about accommodations and what type of clothing to bring; and after packing, unpacking, and packing again she was finally ready. She was going to Africa. Africa! She could hardly believe it herself. She would be working with an organization called Africycle. She had been impressed with their work which was to bring and build refurbished bikes to Malawi in order to help Africans improve the quality of their lives. She had also volunteered to work in two orphanages in two different towns. She wanted very much to help out in any way she could. Of course, she also hoped to do some sightseeing. Lyndsay's mind could hardly contain the things she had planned to do over the next three months, but she would think about that on the plane this evening.

Today, now, was for her mother. She would be meeting her mother for lunch, and she was so looking forward to spending some time with her at their favourite spot. They had celebrated so many occasions at the tea room that it had now become their custom; before and after each marathon; when she got the job and subsequently the promotion at the sports store where she worked; these had all been celebrated there, so it was only fitting to be going today to celebrate her upcoming adventure. Lyndsay glanced at her watch to check the time and felt the faint grumblings of hunger as she thought of her favourite sandwich – the curried tuna salad. It was an unusual combination of white tuna, mild curry, pecans and currants. Yum! She recalled fondly the first time she and her mother had gone to the tea room. The thought of curry had not seemed so appealing at the time, and it was only after their third or fourth visit when her mother had insisted she try a bite of her sandwich, that Lyndsay too had become hooked.

The memory of it put a smile on her face, just as her mother's brave attempt to be lighthearted these last few days put a smile in her heart. Though her mother was her staunchest supporter, Lyndsay sensed the disquiet she was feeling about her trip, and for the first time, she fully understood the strength of the maternal bond. Dear, sweet mother, she would be okay. In fact, she would be just fine.

RECIPES

SANDWICHES

"One of the very nicest things about life is the way we must regularly stop whatever it is we are doing and devote our attention to eating."
Luciano Pavarotti and William Wright
Pavarotti, My Own Story

1. Curried Tuna Sandwich

2. Chicken Salad Sandwich with Lemon Cilantro Aioli

3. Roast Beef Sandwich with Roasted Garlic Mayonnaise

4. Egg Salad Sandwich with Chives

5. Cucumber and Cream Cheese Sandwich

6. Smoked Salmon and Dill Open Faced Sandwich

CURRIED TUNA SANDWICH

This was our most requested sandwich. Something about the sweet/savoury combination of the ingredients made it an instant hit. To those many, many customers who requested the recipe – here it is. Enjoy!

Your choice of sliced bread

2 -184 gram cans solid white tuna, drained
3 tbsp currants
3 tbsp finely chopped pecans
1/3- ½ cup mayonnaise
3 tsp mild curry powder, or to taste
2 tsp brown sugar, optional

- Flake tuna with fork to separate meat.
- Add currants and pecans and stir. Start with 1/3 cup mayonnaise, adding more if you want a creamier texture.
- Add remainder of ingredients and mix well; refrigerate until needed.

Makes 3 – 4 sandwiches.

Making this recipe the day before allows time for the flavours to really develop. It's worth the wait.

CHICKEN SALAD SANDWICH WITH LEMON CILANTRO AIOLI

This is a lively salad, with hints of cayenne and a squirt of lemon to tingle the tongue. Adjust the seasonings if you like something with more bite.

2 boneless, skinless chicken breasts
½ onion
2 cloves garlic
1 bay leaf
Water
Any fresh herbs (parsley or cilantro work well) you have on hand.

½ cup mayonnaise
½ lemon, juice of
3 tbsp chopped fresh cilantro
Pinch cayenne pepper, or to taste
Pinch freshly ground pepper, or to taste.

- In a medium saucepan, poach chicken in water along with onion, garlic, bay leaf and herbs until cooked.
- Remove chicken and discard liquid with herbs or save for another use. (You can freeze the strained liquid and use it for soup stock).
- Dice the chicken finely. Add mayonnaise, lemon juice, fresh cilantro, cayenne and black pepper.
- Stir to combine and adjust seasonings if required.
- Refrigerate until ready to use.

Makes 3 – 4 sandwiches.

ROAST BEEF SANDWICH WITH ROASTED GARLIC MAYONNAISE

Good quality roast beef is essential in this sandwich. Some roast beef varieties at the deli counter are overcooked and dry. I buy an Angus Beef variety that is slightly pink in the centre. Many grocery stores roast their own beef; and these are a better choice.

8 slices of bread, your choice

¼ cup mayonnaise
1 tbsp well drained horseradish
½ tsp Dijon mustard
1 – 2 cloves of roasted garlic, peeled and mashed
8 – 12 slices thinly sliced medium-rare roast beef

- In a small bowl, mix together mayonnaise, horseradish, mustard, and roasted garlic.
- Spread each slice of bread with a thin layer of flavoured mayonnaise.
- Add 2 – 3 slices of roast beef on each of four slices of bread.
- Top each sandwich with remaining bread, mayo side down.

Makes 4 sandwiches.

EGG SALAD SANDWICH WITH CHIVES

You can experiment with other fresh herbs in this recipe. The mayonnaise quantity is only a guideline as some people like their filling more or less creamy.

6 hard boiled eggs, peeled and chopped*
¼ cup mayonnaise
3 tbsp chopped fresh chives
Salt and pepper to taste

* Mix the egg with mayonnaise, fresh herbs and salt and pepper.
* Refrigerate until ready to use.

Makes 3 – 4 sandwiches.

*When I was training my staff, I discovered that most people over cook their hard boiled eggs so that they get that ugly greenish tinge around the yolk. Here are my instructions on how to properly hard cook eggs.

* Place eggs in a pot large enough to hold them comfortably leaving enough space around them so that they don't bump into each other as they boil.
* Cover with cold water and boil over high heat until the eggs come to a roiling boil.
* Turn off the heat and remove pot from hot element onto a cold element and cover with a tight fitting lid.
* Leave the eggs for 15 minutes. They will continue to cook during this time.
* After 15 minutes, drain off the hot water and cover with cold tap water.
* Leave for an additional 15 minutes to cool down.
* Then crack the eggs against the side of the pot, and leave for an additional 15 minutes. This will allow the water to slowly seep into the cracked egg which makes it easier to peel.

CUCUMBER AND CREAM CHEESE SANDWICH

This sandwich is the quintessential 'tea tray' sandwich. It is traditional for the cucumber to be peeled and cut in very thin slices. You can add watercress or fresh basil to these to really pump up the taste. Also try experimenting with a variety of fresh herbs in the cream cheese. A soft, white bread is best for this sandwich.

½ English cucumber, peeled and sliced thinly
125 grams softened cream cheese
Salt and pepper to taste

- Spread cream cheese on each of four slices of bread.
- Top with a thin layer of cucumber slices.
- Sprinkle with salt and pepper to taste.
- Top with remaining bread.

Makes about 4 sandwiches.

SMOKED SALMON AND DILL OPEN FACED SANDWICH

Ideally you want to use a bread with substance for this sandwich; pumpernickel or multigrain are good choices.

8-10 slices smoked salmon
4 slices pumpernickel or multigrain bread
1/3 cup cream cheese, softened
Salt and pepper to taste
Fresh dill sprigs
1 ½ tbsp capers
Lemon

- Spread cream cheese on your choice of bread.
- Divide smoked salmon evenly among bread.
- Sprinkle with drained capers and fresh dill sprigs
- Add salt and pepper to taste.
- Spritz with lemon juice.

Makes 4 servings

Chapter Seven
Reminiscence
Desserts

The girls were meeting today for Kaffee Stunde. Phone calls were made, and calendars cleared for this very important appointment.

It had all started with Gisela, who, with her German background and her love of sweets had introduced this tradition to the group. Kaffee Stunde, literally translated, means coffee hour. Like the British tradition of tea and biscuits in the afternoon, the Germans and Viennese love to take a break at around four in the afternoon to share a sweet something with friends. At first, it was just a comment that Gisela made whenever any one of the group had had a particularly trying day, "Okay, it's time for a Kaffee Stunde" she'd say. It was like the magic bullet that would chase away the stresses of the day. The expression flew from her lips so often that soon the other women began repeating it. It became a catch phrase between them – called upon whether celebrating or commiserating. At first, they would meet informally at each other's homes, to share whatever hot liquid or sweet treat was handy, and to give themselves a much needed break, a little respite from children and housework. When they were together the little catastrophes of the day would somehow be diminished to comedic events. Soon, they were meeting every week or so; whenever time allowed. It so solidified the friendship between the women that now it was not only Kaffee Stunde that they shared between them, but also movie nights, and swim evenings, cottage getaways and shopping trips.

With the kids mostly grown and gone, the original handful of women had swollen to twice that size. Though the ten or so women were rarely all present at any one Kaffee Stunde, usually within the space of a month everyone had met and caught up with one another. And, though it sometimes seemed to the various spouses just a frivolous time with friends, the group was loyal to each other. Through parents' death, marriage break-ups, business failings, and ill health, they had each others' backs at all times. If they needed help with something, they called on one of the girls. Often, help came along unbidden. Such was the strength of their friendship.

And today, they were all meeting at Tempest in a Teapot for their ritual. When they met at the Tempest, as they sometimes did, it was something of a homecoming, for the owner was one of them. It was to this group that she first shared her dream of a tea room, and it was this group that helped her with the painting and the hauling when she first opened her business; and she, in return, kept them well supplied with their favourite tea, stories of her frustrations and of her sometimes zany customers.

The table had been reserved for three o'clock. Though everyone was always invited, they never knew exactly how many of them were able to make it. Consequently, they were never able to give an exact number of seats when reserving, it was always a range —"between six to eight", or sometimes "nine or ten". It was all very confusing and this sometimes posed problems with some establishments, but it never stressed the girls; if more showed up, they just squeezed in a little tighter. If less showed up, they took it all in stride, as they did most things. The first to arrive, on this day, was Michele, the realtor. She was a long-legged, brown haired woman with soft brown eyes and an easy disposition. Always a kind word for everyone, she had a sense of humour that often took people by surprise. Because it was a small community, and she and her husband were one of the leading realtors in the area, she knew everyone and everyone knew her. Consequently, wherever Michele found herself, she was certain to know several people; many of them past clients, and always took the time to chat with them. After a quick hello and hug to Sara, the owner, who was in the front gift shoppe with customers, Michele made her way through the arbour, and into the tea room proper. She spied two people she knew, and walked over to say hello while she waited for the others to appear. As she chatted, she glanced at the blackboard to see what the dessert of the day was – Citrus Chiffon cake served with orange sorbet. Would she have her usual Sticky Date Pudding, or try the special?

Susan and Heather arrived almost simultaneously. Having met in the parking lot, they walked together to the tea room, talking nonstop. They were both hoping that everyone would be on time today. Because they worked full time; Susan at the local seniors' residence and Heather at the optometrist office, their schedules were not as flexible as some of the other women, and were consequently always checking their watches. Today, they were both working late shifts; so it had been possible for them to take their lunch at three o'clock in order to meet up with the group. Susan had a soft, lilting British accent and short blond hair. She was perhaps the shyest in the group, the least likely to share her innermost feelings; consequently, the group had been surprised some years back when she quietly told them that her marriage had ended. They were enormously fond of her, and respected her privacy, so they didn't ask a lot of questions as to the whys and wherefores, but waited patiently until Susan was ready to talk about it. They knew it would take awhile.

Heather, on the other hand, was not quiet and shy. She was quick witted, outspoken, and confident. Ready to share her opinion on almost any subject, she kept the group entertained with her scathing opinion of politicians and other government employees. Of course, unionized or otherwise 'privileged and protected' workers were her personal favourites to pick upon. Her mantra was always, "they should try getting a job in the real world". Agree with her or not, discussions with Heather were never boring. A quick wave to Sara, who was measuring out tea for a customer, and they too, walked through the arbour and into the tea room. They caught Michele's eye; she graciously bid adieu to the elderly couple she had been talking to, and walked across to the waiting table. After hugs and kisses, the three took their seats and got down to the business of ordering tea. Heather quickly glanced at the board and hoped that the Crème Brulee was the classic today. They sometimes changed up the flavour of this perennial favourite, but Heather always preferred the classic vanilla. Sue debated whether to have a sandwich; this was after all her lunch break, or go straight to dessert - the Cream Tea or the Bread Pudding were always good choices.

Melody appeared just as Carolyn, the server, was delivering pots of steaming hot tea to the three women. She had short, wavy blond hair, riveting blue eyes and was a powerhouse of activity. Besides working out at the gym three days a week, Melody played tennis, baseball, worked at the tea room part time and kept the books for her husband's company, amid a myriad of other social commitments. The other girls who worked with her often wondered how she managed to find the time to work at all. Melody sailed through the tea room, waving as she went, and made her way directly to the kitchen. She exchanged a quick hello to Janette, who ran the kitchen, grabbed herself a mug, which she preferred to a cup and saucer; then sat herself down at the table with the others. Whenever the group met at the Tempest they were always careful to plan these outings on a day when Melody wasn't working. It would not do to have her waiting on other tables while this particular group was in; she would miss vital parts of the conversation, and consequently the others would spend too much time repeating and recounting things. Once, when the group did come in while Melody was working, they all made exaggerated demands on her, had her running back and forth, then left her a penny tip as a joke. They all still laughed over it. Today, Melody wondered whether she could talk Michele into sharing a Sticky Date Pudding with her. She thought about this for some time; then considered that she had worked out this morning, and was playing baseball tonight. Perhaps she could afford to splurge on a whole dessert.

The last to arrive, this particular day, was Gisela. Though she was often the event planner, she was most likely to be the last to arrive. She claimed that she had the furthest to travel since she had moved out of town several years before; but the girls were quick to remind her that she had always been last to arrive, even when she lived ten minutes away. She good naturedly agreed with this each time. They always poked fun at the fact that Gisela had to be perfectly coiffed and perfectly matched before she left the house, this, they claimed was the real reason she was constantly late. She did not dispute this either. She was undoubtedly the perfectionist in the group. The others were secretly jealous of this skill she had to clean, organize, and colour co-ordinate everything that crossed her path. Gisela, for her part, couldn't really understand why this didn't come naturally to everyone. "Come on, get with the program," she was often heard saying.

The girls were already enjoying their tea and discussing the merits of their favourite dessert, when Gisela took her seat. She noted that there was one empty spot at the table, as none of the others had been able to make it today, and knew that the spot would be filled by Sara who would join them between customers. A few minutes later, Sara, free at last, came by to officially say hello. She was always happy to see the girls, and noted with affection, that this was the original six. With the exception of Linda, who had moved to Kelowna, this was the group that started it all fifteen years ago. Who would have guessed, back then, that their lives would still be intertwined? Where had all the time gone? One thing for sure, thought Sara, the group was just as loud today as it had been back then. She looked around the table as everyone was talking and laughing noisily, gesticulating with their hands to make a particular point, or exclaiming out loud at a surprise comment. No, this was decidedly not a quiet, sedate group. She would have to get their attention so that they could order dessert, as she knew some of them were on a tight schedule.

"So, who's up for Kaffee Stunde?" she asked loudly. Everybody stopped what they were doing and gave Sara their undivided attention.

She wondered, not for the first time, why they bothered with a menu. They knew exactly what they wanted, and so did she. "Heather, you'll have the Crème Brulee? It's classic today." She stopped to acknowledge a nod; then continued. "Sue, the Bread Pudding?" Gisela – Carrot Cake for you? And I guess the only real question is whether Melody and Michele will have their own or share a Sticky Date Pudding?"

Melody and Michele looked at each other briefly, gave up all pretense of considering sharing, then answered in unison, "our own, please, with…"

"….with lots of caramel sauce," finished Sara with a laugh.

"And what will you have, Sara?" wondered Michele.

"I haven't even had my lunch yet," she answered.

"Lunch? Lunch?" asked Gisela, with mock indignation. "This is a Kaffee Stunde, get with the program." Everyone burst into loud laughter.

"No, definitely not a quiet group," thought Sara as she made her way to the kitchen to place the order.

She wouldn't have it any other way.

RECIPES

DESSERTS

"Life is uncertain. Eat dessert first."

Ernestine Ulmer

1. Sticky Date Pudding with Caramel Sauce

2. Bread Pudding

3. Carrot Cake with Citrus Cream Cheese Frosting

4. Chocolate Raspberry Torte with Raspberry Coulis

5. Vanilla Cheesecake

6. Classic Crème Brulee

7. Citrus Chiffon Cake

8. Almond Plum Cake

9. Bavarian Apple Torte

10. Apple Cranberry Crumble

STICKY DATE PUDDING WITH CARAMEL SAUCE

We baked up these favourite cakes in individual bundt trays (6 small cakes to a pan). As most people may not have individual bundt cake trays, instructions are given for an 8 inch square baking pan. These need to be baked in a water bath.

1 ¾ cups packed, pitted dates (about 10 oz), coarsely chopped
2 cups water
1 ½ tsp baking soda
2 cups all-purpose flour
½ tsp baking powder
½ tsp ground ginger
½ tsp salt
1/3 cup unsalted butter, softened
1 cup granulated sugar
3 eggs

Preheat oven to 375° F.
- Butter and lightly flour an 8 inch square baking pan.
- In a saucepan, simmer dates in water, uncovered, for about 5 minutes or until soft.
- Remove from heat; stir in baking soda. (Mixture will foam). Let stand 20 minutes.
- In a medium mixing bowl, combine flour, baking powder, ginger and salt.
- In a large bowl with electric mixer, beat together the butter and sugar until light and fluffy. Beat in eggs, one at a time; beating well after each addition.
- Add flour mixture in 3 batches, beating after each addition just until combined.
- Stir in date mixture with a wooden spoon until well mixed.
- Pour batter into prepared pan and set pan in a larger pan. Add enough water to larger pan to reach halfway up sides of smaller pan. Bake 35 – 40 minutes or until tester comes out clean. Cool on wire rack.
- Cut in 9 pieces.

*If you do happen to have individual bundt pans, this recipe will make 10 individual cakes, adjust baking time to about 20 – 25 minutes.

Caramel Sauce

This recipe will give you more caramel sauce then you need for the sticky date pudding recipe. Enjoy leftovers with ice cream!

1 cup unsalted butter
½ cup honey
1 cup packed brown sugar
½ cup whipped cream
1 tsp vanilla extract

- In heavy saucepan over medium heat, melt butter; honey and brown sugar. Stir until sugar dissolves.
- Over medium- high; bring to a boil, stirring occasionally.
- Stir in cream and vanilla extract, then let boil again without stirring, until thickened slightly, about 5 minutes.
- Serve warm over pudding.

Makes about 2 ½ cups sauce.

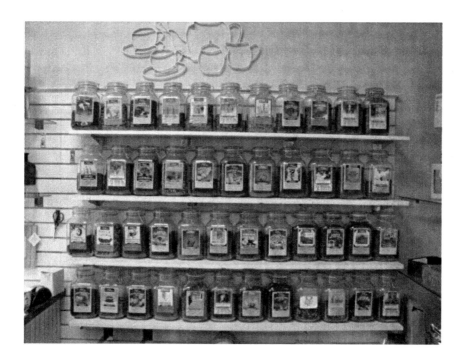

BREAD PUDDING

Most bread pudding recipes call for French bread or any type of firm day old white bread. I have found that egg breads, challah, brioche, or plain Italian panettone offer a richer taste. This is also a very versatile dish. Try sautéing apples or pears with butter and brown sugar and add to the bread cubes for a totally different taste sensation.

10 cups day old, cubed bread
8 large eggs, at room temperature
1 1/2 cups sugar
4 cups milk
1½ tsp cinnamon
1 tsp vanilla
1/3 cup dried cranberries or raisons
Grated zest of one orange

Preheat oven to 350° F.
• Lightly grease a 9 x 13 baking pan. Spread the bread cubes in it. Sprinkle raisons or cranberries over top
• In a bowl, whisk together the eggs, milk, sugar, vanilla, cinnamon and orange zest until well combined.
• Pour the mixture over the bread cubes. Let sit, pressing down on the bread occasionally, until the bread is evenly soaked, about 10 minutes.
• Place baking pan in a larger pan with shallow sides.
• Add very hot tap water to the larger pan until it comes half way up sides of smaller pan.
• Bake until knife inserted in centre comes out almost clean, 45 - 55 minutes.
• Serve warm or at room temperature with custard or caramel sauce.

Makes 9 servings.

CARROT CAKE WITH CITRUS CREAM CHEESE FROSTING

This is one of the nicest carrot cake recipes I have come across. The citrus in the cream cheese gives it a lighter, more contemporary taste.

2 cups all purpose flour
1 ½ tsp baking powder
½ tsp baking soda
1 tsp cinnamon
½ tsp nutmeg
¼ tsp ground clove or allspice
½ tsp salt
¾ cup unsalted butter, softened
½ cup honey
2 eggs
1 cup granulated sugar
1 tsp vanilla
3 cups finely grated carrot
1 apple, peeled and grated

Preheat oven to 350° F.
• Butter two 9 inch round cake pans; line bottom with parchment paper.
• In a medium mixing bowl, combine flour, baking powder, baking soda, spices and salt.
• In a bowl, using electric mixer, cream butter until light and fluffy.
• Slowly beat in honey, then eggs, one at a time.
• Beat in sugar and vanilla.
• Add flour mixture to butter mixture in three additions, stirring until just absorbed. Stir in carrots and apple.
• Divide batter evenly between pans; smooth tops.
• Bake in centre of oven for 25 – 30 minutes or until cake tester inserted in centre comes out clean.
• Cool on rack for 10 minutes. Remove from pans.

Frosting
1 250g package cream cheese, at room temperature
½ cup unsalted butter, softened
2 tbsp honey
2 tbsp finely grated orange, lemon or lime zest (or a mixture of all three)
2 tsp lemon juice

4 – 5 cups sifted icing sugar

- Beat cream cheese with electric mixer until smooth.
- Gradually beat in butter, then honey, zest and lemon juice.
- Gradually add icing sugar until thick enough for spreading.

To assemble cake:

Spread frosting between cake layers, then over sides and top. Sprinkle with extra zest if desired.

Makes 12 servings.

CHOCOLATE RASPBERRY TORTE

This is a rich, moist cake. You can use semisweet chocolate instead of the bittersweet if you wish, but the bittersweet offers a depth of flavour that the semisweet chocolate can't match!

5½ oz bittersweet chocolate, chopped
3 oz unsweetened chocolate, chopped
2/3 cup unsalted butter, cut into small pieces
7 tbsp seedless raspberry jam
4 large eggs, at room temperature
¾ cup granulated sugar
1 tbsp raspberry flavoured liqueur (Framboise)
½ cup plus 1 tbsp all purpose flour
¾ tsp baking powder
¼ tsp salt

Preheat oven to 350° F.
• Grease a 9 inch round cake pan and line bottom with parchment paper. Grease the paper and dust the insides of pan with flour, tapping out the excess. Set aside.
• Place a large pot on the stove with about 1 ½ inches of water in the bottom, and bring to just below a gentle simmer. Combine the chopped chocolates and the butter in a stainless steel or glass bowl and set this over the barely simmering water. Melt the mixture, stirring occasionally. When the mixture is almost melted, add the raspberry jam and turn off the heat. Stir until smooth. Let cool.
• In a small bowl, sift together the flour, baking powder and salt; set aside.
• In a large bowl, beat the eggs and sugar until mixture is thick and pale and falls from the whisk or beaters in a ribbon when lifted. Beat in the Framboise.
• Beat the cooled chocolate mixture into the egg mixture, until well blended.
• Fold in the sifted flour mixture; then scrape the batter into the prepared pan.
• Bake until top is cracked in several places, and a tester inserted in centre of cake comes out clean, about 40 – 45 minutes. Transfer to wire rack and cool 10 minutes.
• Run a knife around the edge of cake and invert onto a rack. Carefully peel off the parchment paper and cool completely.

Syrup
½ cup granulated sugar
1 tbsp light corn syrup
¼ cup water
¼ cup Framboise

• In a small, heavy bottomed saucepan, combine sugar, corn syrup and water. Stir over medium-low heat until sugar dissolves, then increase heat and bring to a boil. Boil for 30 seconds, then remove from heat and let cool for 5 minutes. Add the liqueur and let cool completely before brushing on cake.
• The syrup will help to keep the cake moist and fresh for several days at room temperature. Serve with raspberry coulis.

Raspberry Coulis:

2 pkgs (10 oz each) frozen, unsweetened raspberries
thawed overnight in refrigerator or 3 cups fresh raspberries
¼ to ½ cups sugar
2 tbsp Framboise

• If using frozen raspberries, drain, reserving the liquid. Place the berries and ¼ cup reserved juice in a food processor and add ¼ cup sugar.
• Whir the berries until pureed, adding more juice if the puree seems too thick. Add the liqueur, then taste for sweetness and add more sugar if necessary.

This sauce is also wonderful over angel food cake or ice cream.

VANILLA CHEESECAKE

This cheesecake recipe is one of the richest tasting we have found. It calls for vanilla extract, but we use a vanilla bean as it not only adds wonderful little specks throughout the batter, but the taste is far superior. When you have scraped out the beans, don't throw out the pods. Place them in your sugar bowl for wonderfully fragrant vanilla sugar to enhance your coffee or tea.

For the crust:
1 ½ cups graham cracker crumbs
3 tbsp sugar
½ tsp ground cinnamon
¼ cup unsalted butter, melted, plus extra for greasing

Preheat oven to 400° F.
• Lightly grease a 9 inch springform pan. In a bowl, combine graham cracker crumbs, sugar, cinnamon and melted butter. Stir until well blended and evenly moist. Pour into springform pan and press evenly onto bottom and about 1 ½ inch up sides of pan.
• Bake until lightly golden and set, about 10 minutes. Cool completely.
• Reduce oven temperature to 300 degrees.

Filling:
4 pkgs (250g each) cream cheese, at room temperature
2 tbsp all purpose flour
¼ tsp salt
1 ¼ cups sugar
½ cup sour cream
1 tbsp vanilla extract or ½ vanilla bean, scraped
3 large eggs, at room temperature

• In a large bowl using mixer at medium-high speed, combine cream cheese, flour and salt. Beat until very smooth and fluffy, scraping down sides of bowl.
• Add sugar, sour cream and vanilla. Beat until well blended, again scraping down sides of bowl. Add the eggs, one at a time, beating well after each addition.
• Pour mixture into the cooled crust.

- Bake in 300 degree oven for 60 – 70 minutes or until filling is set and edges are slightly puffed. The centre will be slightly wobbly. The filling will firm as it cools.
- Cover and refrigerate until well chilled.

Makes 12 servings.

CLASSIC CRÈME BRULEE

You will need six ½ cup ramekins for this recipe. You can freeze the eggs whites from this recipe and use them later to make the Citrus Chiffon cake recipe provided in this book. Remember to label and date the egg whites before storing in the freezer. Defrost overnight in the refrigerator before using them.

1½ cups whipping cream
½ cup milk
¼ cup granulated sugar
1 tbsp vanilla extract or ½ vanilla bean
6 egg yolks
¼ cup granulated sugar
2 tbsp granulated sugar.

Preheat oven to 300 º F.

• In a saucepan over medium heat, combine cream, milk, ¼ cup sugar and vanilla; cook, stirring until sugar dissolves. Remove from heat.

• In a bowl, whisk egg yolks with ¼ cup sugar; gradually whisk in hot cream mixture. Pour mixture back into saucepan; cook over low heat a few minutes, stirring constantly, until slightly thickened. Pour into ramekins.

• Set ramekins in a pan large enough to hold them; pour enough hot water to come half way up sides. Bake 40 – 50 minutes or until almost set. They should be slightly wobbly in centre. Remove from water bath; cool on wire racks. Chill.

To brulee, set top oven rack as close to element as possible and preheat broiler. Sprinkle 1 tsp sugar over top of each custard. Cook until sugar melts then caramelizes. Watch these closely. Alternatively use brulee torch and caramelize each custard individually. Serve immediately.

CITRUS CHIFFON CAKE

This light cake is worthy of being eaten without guilt. Weighing the flour and sugar guarantees a billowy cake. It is wonderful served with orange sorbet or raspberry coulis.

1 ½ tsp baking powder
½ tsp salt
8 oz granulated sugar (about 1 cup, divided)
6 oz sifted cake flour (about 1 ¾ cups)
1 tbsp grated orange rind
½ cup fresh orange juice (about one orange)
1 tbsp grated lemon rind
5 tbsp canola oil
1 ½ tsp vanilla extract
3 large egg yolks
6 large egg whites
¾ tsp cream of tartar
2 tsp powdered sugar

Preheat oven to 325 º F.
• Combine baking powder, salt, 7 ounces sugar, and flour in a large bowl, stirring with a whisk until mixture is well combined.
• Combine orange rind and next 5 ingredients (through egg yolks) in a medium bowl, stirring with a whisk. Add rind mixture to flour mixture, stirring until smooth.
• Place egg whites in a large bowl; beat with a mixer at high speed until foamy. Add cream of tartar; beat until soft peaks form. Gradually add remaining 1 ounce sugar and continue beating until stiff peaks forms.
• Gently stir one quarter of egg white mixture into flour mixture; gently fold in remaining egg white mixture.
• Spoon batter into ungreased 10 inch tube pan, spreading evenly. Break air pockets by cutting through batter with a knife. Bake for 45 minutes or until cake springs back when lightly touched. Invert pan; cool completely. Loosen cake from sides of pan using a narrow metal spatula. Invert cake onto plate. Sift powdered sugar over top of cake.

Makes 12 servings.

ALMOND PLUM CAKE

This is a wonderfully rustic cake with lots of great flavour.

½ cup whole almonds, finely ground
1 ½ cups all purpose flour
1 tsp baking powder
¼ tsp salt
1 cup unsalted butter, at room temperature
1 cup, plus 4 tsp sugar
2 large eggs
1 tsp vanilla extract
½ tsp almond extract
1 ¼ lbs plums (about 8 medium) pitted, halved, cut into ½ inch thick slices
¾ tsp cinnamon

Preheat oven to 350ºF.
• Spray a 9 inch round cake pan with non stick cooking spray, or lightly butter. Line bottom of pan with parchment paper.
• In a medium bowl; whisk flour, baking powder, and salt.
• In a large bowl with electric mixer, beat butter until fluffy; add 1 cup sugar until well blended. Add eggs 1 at a time beating well after each addition. Beat in vanilla and almond extract. Add flour mixture just until combined.
• Transfer batter to prepared pan; spread evenly and smooth top with spatula. Gently press plum slices, flesh side down, into batter in spoke pattern around outer rim and centre of cake placing close together.
• Mix cinnamon and 4 tsp sugar in small bowl, sprinkle over plums.
• Bake cake until tester inserted in centre comes out clean, about 50 minutes. Cool cake in pan on rack 20 minutes. Run small knife between cake and pan sides to loosen. Invert cake onto platter; remove parchment paper. Placing another plate over cake, carefully invert unto another plate, plum side up. Cool cake completely.

Makes 8 servings.

BAVARIAN APPLE TORTE

This is a family favourite. It combines the flavour of apple pie and the creaminess of cheesecake in one dish. Who could ask for anything more?

Base
1/2 cup unsalted butter, at room temperature
1/3 cup granulated sugar
¼ tsp vanilla extract
1 cup all purpose flour
¼ cup raspberry jam

Filling
250 g package cream cheese, at room temperature
¼ cup granulated sugar
1 egg
½ tsp vanilla extract

Topping
1/3 cup granulated sugar
½ tsp cinnamon
4 apples, peeled, cored and sliced
½ cup sliced almonds

Preheat oven to 450ºF.
• To make crust, cream butter, sugar and vanilla. Blend in flour. Press on the bottom and sides of a 9 inch springform pan. Spread with a thin layer of raspberry jam.
• For the filling, combine the cream cheese and sugar. Add the egg and vanilla; mix well. Pour over jam.
• For the topping, toss the apples with the sugar and cinnamon and spoon over the cream cheese mixture. Sprinkle with the sliced almonds.
• Bake at 450ºF for 10 minutes, then 400ºF for 25 minutes. Cool and carefully remove sides of pan. Refrigerate until needed.

Makes 8 – 10 servings.

APPLE CRANBERRY CRUMBLE

Crisps and crumbles are amazingly versatile. Try substituting pears for the apples and dried cherries for the cranberries. If using fresh cranberries, use one cup.

Topping
¾ cup all purpose flour
¾ cup old fashioned rolled oats
¾ cup firmly packed brown sugar
¾ cup cold unsalted butter, cut in small pieces

Filling
Seeds of 1 plump vanilla bean
¼ cup firmly packed brown sugar
¼ cup granulated sugar
½ tbsp cornstarch
5 to 6 medium apples
½ cup dried cranberries

Preheat oven to 375°F.
• Butter an 8 by 11 inch baking dish.
• Combine the flour, oats, brown sugar and butter in a mixing bowl and cut together until the butter pieces are about the size of the oats.
• In a large bowl, stir together the vanilla seeds, sugars, cornstarch and cinnamon. Peel and core the apples and cut them into rough slices or chunks. Add the apples and cranberries to the sugar and cinnamon mixture and toss to coat evenly.
• Place the fruit mixture in the baking dish and top with oat mixture, distributing it evenly.
• Bake for about 45 minutes or until the topping is crisp and golden and the filling can be seen bubbling. Cool at least 15 minutes before serving or serve at room temperature.
• Serve with custard or ice cream.

Makes 6 – 8 servings.

Chapter Eight
Reminiscence
Beginnings and Endings

"Our life is an apprenticeship to the truth that around every circle another can be drawn; that there is no end in nature, but every end is a beginning..."

Ralph Waldo Emerson

Sara pulled the chain on the electric 'open' sign in the display window and watched as the neon brightness vanished in a blink. She walked over to the door, turned over the sign that hung there to the 'closed' position and locked the door. It had been an exhausting day, and Sara felt it in her neck and shoulders, always the central point in her body that seemed to accumulate all the tension and stresses of the day.

The staff had all gone home and everything was quiet, clean and tidy. A sense of sadness and dejection seemed to hang in the air. Today had been the last day of business in the tea room of Tempest in a Teapot. Though the store would likely remain open for several more weeks to sell off the remaining inventory in the gift shoppe, it was the tea room that held the greatest pride, and conversely, the greatest frustration for Sara, and it was the tea room's loss that she was feeling the most this day.

She had opened the business five years earlier, after eight years of nurturing the idea in her head, years of waiting for two sons to be a bit older and more independent, years of trying to persuade her more cautious husband that it was a venture worth pursuing. It had been in her head for so long now, that it felt like a third child. She recalled the day, five and a half years ago, when her husband had finally given his endorsement to go ahead with it. She had been disbelieving at first, then jubilant that her dream was finally about to come true. And what an adventure it had been! Finding a location, then planning it all out (though in truth it had already been all planned out in her head), it had been such fun. There had certainly been challenges along the way, from turning a decrepit location into a welcoming spot, to scrambling to obtain the often contradictory information regarding permits and licenses. She recalled her biggest challenge – the day almost four years ago, when a torrential rain storm had partially collapsed the flat roof of the building. This caused a great gush of water to come through the floor of the vacant apartment upstairs onto the unsuspecting heads of her customers as they sat sipping their tea. The insurance company had refused to cover her losses as the landlord had, unbeknownst to her, past problems that had gone unheeded and unattended. Failing to recoup her costs with the landlord directly, the frustration and anger that followed had catapulted her to never again be at the mercy of ignorant, absentee landlords who were content to see their investments fall into ruin, rather than inject some of the money they had been reaping for years into keeping their properties up to standard. That's when she and her husband had decided to buy a small property on Main Street to house their slowly growing business with an eye to the future.

Sara was a dreamer in many ways, and it was this quality in her that had prompted her to start the business. But she was also a realist, and she always knew, right from the start, that there was a chance of failure. In the fifteen years since her family had moved to this town, she had watched with interest the many businesses that had set up shop along the main street, only to close their doors a year or two afterward. This town was, in many ways, a tough nut to crack, retail wise. Just a little too close to the retail malls of the neighbouring towns, it had always been a challenge to convince the residents that they should shop locally. The town had its roots in farming, and as such, many of the long time residents were by nature careful with their money and were not given to indulgences. She knew that the opening of the 'big box' outlet south of Main Street had not helped. They sold the same mugs, teapots, candles and other small decorative items at far less than she could, often at the same price that her wholesale supplier were charging her. She supposed it was pointless to speculate on just why her sales had taken a hit.

The reality was that people shopped for price, and that had really been the deciding factor in her decision to close.

The gift shoppe had, right from the beginning, subsidized the cost of operating the tea room, where the cost of food and labour were quite high. Sara had always had a love of cooking and baking, and so had insisted on using the freshest ingredients to hand make all the items on the menu. She had no interest in offering foods that were easily available in other eateries, foods that were prepared in some large commercial plant, using imitation ingredients. She was a purist when it came to foods and had insisted on real cream, real butter, real everything. You could not dispute the difference when you flavoured crème brulee with vanilla beans instead of artificial vanilla extract – one was ordinary, the other sublime. It was this passion and commitment to real food that had dissuaded her, in the end, from trying to continue the business by cutting costs in the tea room either with the food or with the staffing. There was a certain stubbornness in her; if she could not, at the end of the day, do something or produce something that she was proud of; then she would not do it at all.

It simply came down to declining sales and rising costs. After crunching the numbers, it became obvious that it would be more financially astute to lease the building to another business than to continue to run her business under the circumstances. Sara knew she had a small, loyal and dedicated following, and it was for them she felt sad today. She knew that they had loved coming there, knew that they would miss the place terribly. She had been moved by the many thank you cards and flowers she had received from appreciative customers. She glanced at the assortment of cards on the glass shelf behind the desk and smiled. She would miss them, too.

Sara walked through to the kitchen, made herself a mug of ginger tea, and returned to the tea room, where she sat down at the corner table. She had always enjoyed this time at the end of the day, when everyone had gone and the place was freshly cleaned, awaiting another day. She stirred her tea slowly and looked lovingly at the spot she had created; at all the tea quotes she had painstakingly hand painted on the walls, at the ivy topped arbour that would now grace her garden, and she was at peace. Though the tea room would not welcome another day, and Sara was happy to be leaving the frustrations of operating a business, she was uppermost happy to have had the opportunity to be part of this special place. Truly, she had no regrets. She had gained a wealth of knowledge during the last five or so years, and made a wealth of friends. At the end of the day, it had been a worthy journey.

There is no trouble so
great or grave that cannot
be much diminished by a
nice cup of tea.

Bernard-Paul Heroux

Tea urges
tranquillity
of the soul.

Henry Wadsworth Longfellow

Ceylon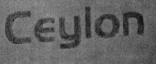

Epilogue
What next?

It is not everyday that people get to realize their life long dream, and I feel truly blessed that I was able to do this twice. My dream of opening and operating a tea room has been one of the most rewarding experiences of my life, and though it was not entirely a bed of roses, (and some would say that it was not a successful venture) I have no regrets. Most gratifying to me was the acknowledgement my customers gave me of their enjoyment of the tea room, and especially the food. It was their constant request for recipes that led me to realize my second dream, which was to write a book. An avid reader since I was a child, I had always flirted with the idea of writing a book. Though this is mainly a cook book, I thank you for indulging me in my effort to write. What a wonderful way to celebrate, and ultimately to close, this chapter of my life. A firm believer in the concept of 'when one door closes, another opens', I am so looking forward to the next chapter.

If you have a dream, I urge you to go for it! For it is in dreams that we are who we were meant to me. I quote Henry David Thoreau, who said, "*I have learned, that if one advances confidently in the direction of his dreams, and endeavors to live the life he has imagined, he will meet with a success unexpected in common hours.*"

For my part, I will be working on growing my online tea business and I will continue to enjoy fragrant cups of steaming tea, while I continue to make and share all the wonderful recipes in this book with friends and family. I will always search out and take pleasure from tea rooms, wherever I may find them – and I wish for you to do the same.

If you are interested in tasting some of the wonderful teas discussed in this book, you can order them through **tempestinateapot.ca.**

Sara Marsala

Printed in the United States
130919LV00002B/8/P

9 780595 515738